by John Persinos

Published by:
Larstan Publishing Inc.
10604 Outpost Dr., N. Potomac, MD 20878
240-396-0007 ext. 901
www.larstan.com

© 2006, Larstan Publishing Inc. All rights reserved. Reproduction of any portion of this book is permitted for individual use if credit is given to John Persinos and Larstan Publishing. Systematic or multiple reproduction or distribution of any part of this book or inclusion of material in publications for sale is permitted only with prior written permission of Larstan Publishing, Inc.

PRINTED IN THE UNITED STATES OF AMERICA

Design by Rob Hudgins & 5050Design.com
Cover design by Mike Gibson
ISBN, Print Edition 978-0-9764266-7-7
Library of Congress Control Number: 2006902942
First Edition

This book is designed to provide accurate and authoritative information on the topic of marketing to the media. It is sold with the understanding that neither the Author nor the Publisher are engaged in rendering any professional or consulting services by publishing this book. As each individual situation is unique, questions relevant to media marketing should be addressed to an appropriate professional to ensure that the situation has been evaluated carefully and appropriately. The Authors and Publisher specifically disclaim any liability, loss or risk which is incurred as a consequence, directly or indirectly, of the use and application of any of the contents of this work.

THE CONFESSIONS OF AN INK-STAINED WRETCH

1 THE MEDIA BORG 21
Examination of interrelated trends, including the rise of the Internet, the decline of local newspapers, the accelerated daily (and intraday) news cycle and the continued consolidation of media ownership. How to make these profound changes work for your marketing/PR message.

2 SWEETHEART, GET ME REWRITE 41
A glimpse at the daily realities of the press, from the author's long experience as a journalist. What it's actually like to work in a bustling newsroom or editorial department, and how this reality applies to your marketing/promotional needs. How to cut through the white noise and get a busy editor's attention. Tailoring your message to the targeted publication.

3 YOU BURIED THE LEDE — AGAIN! 61
The most effective, attention-getting way to write a press release or marketing piece. The language, style and structure to employ to capture an editor's "mind share" and garner coverage. Memorable lessons from the author's days in newsrooms and journalism classrooms.

4 ALL ABOARD THE GRAVY TRAIN 79
The right way to conduct press conferences and events, to get attention for your message. How to promote live events to ensure maximum coverage. The dos and don'ts of event planning — from where and when to schedule it, how to field questions and the right "bait" for reporters.

THE CONFESSIONS OF AN INK-STAINED WRETCH

5 THE RISE OF THE PUNDITOCRACY 93
Examination of the preeminence of cable news and the partisan media. How print, web and cable media intersect, and how to get your message into this integrated news stream. Getting invited to a talk show, the best ways to comport yourself and how to get invited back.

6 OPEN MOUTH, EXTRACT FOOT 107
A guide for top managers on how to handle media interviews, from the perspective of the author, who has interviewed dozens of CEOs and government officials. How to influence the direction of any article. Getting the interview scheduled and making sure it gets prominent play.

7 BARBARIANS AT THE GATE 121
Examines the emergence and growing influence of the Web-based alternative press: bloggers, podcasters and the rest of their ilk. Ways in which the "New Media" have affected conventional media, and the best ways to reach and influence these "game changers." How to become a game changer yourself.

8 THE LAST PLANTATION 143
Explanation of the daily workings of a congressional press office, from the author's perspective as a former congressional press secretary. How to get a member of Congress on board with your message. Why many members simply "run in place," and how to capitalize on these capital follies.

9 ON THE ROAD TO...WHERE? 157
Likely press trends of the future: continued consolidation; diminished media diversity; accelerated decline of newspapers; etc. The implications of these trends on social participation and democracy. How to prepare for these unavoidable developments and exploit them.

www.inkstainedconfessions.com

THE CONFESSIONS OF AN INK-STAINED WRETCH

THE TEAM

Editorial Director | John Persinos
Copy Editor | Tom Scarlett
Contributing Editor | Jonathan Holasek
Creative Director | Rob Hudgins

Group Publisher, Book Division | Eric S. Green
COO | Stan Genkin
CEO | Larry Genkin

LARSTAN PUBLISHING

www.inkstainedconfessions.com

THE CONFESSIONS OF AN INK-STAINED WRETCH

ACKNOWLEDGEMENTS

One of the worst sins in life is ingratitude, an axiom that compels me to write these acknowledgements.

For starters, I thank my parents, Lucas and Maria, for instilling in me an abiding love of reading and the written word. My father and mother also happen to be the kindest people I know. My brother and sister, Tom and Kristen, deserve credit for putting up with me. I'm the oldest — and arguably, the most arrogant — of the three siblings. I cherish Tom and Kristen, more than they know. And a tip of the hat to my aunt, Dr. Georgia Persinos Perdue, whose search in the Amazonian rainforest for cancer cures inspired me as a child to pursue goals larger than myself.

I also thank my beautiful wife, Carole, who is burdened with the most thankless of all occupations — writer's spouse. I appreciate her unflagging support, love and patience. I'd be lost without her.

I also thank Tom Scarlett, who served as copy editor of this book. Tom is a truly brilliant man, but more importantly, he's a loyal friend. His skillful help was invaluable.

My Larstan colleagues, of course, were instrumental in making this book a reality. Mike Wiebner has been my advocate and booster for many years. I'm always touched by his unwavering faith in my abilities; I continually strive to prove that his faith is not misplaced. Eric Green helped pave the way, by managing our book division with professionalism, discipline and a much-welcomed sense of humor. And Rob Hudgins, our talented graphic designer, did a superb job of laying out the book.

THE CONFESSIONS OF AN INK-STAINED WRETCH

Profound gratitude also is in order for Larry Genkin, Larstan's founder and CEO. Larry politely but persistently nagged me, for years, to write a full-fledged book. He provided the corporate resources to make it possible. Larry possesses uncommon decency, compassion and integrity. I'm proud to say that he's one of my closest and most trusted friends. Meanwhile, his father and business partner, Stan, defines the meaning of the word "gentleman."

And finally, I give a warm "thank you" to my daughter, Jennifer. She is the deepest inspiration for all of my personal and professional endeavors. For me, the sun rises and sets with her.

John Persinos

THE CONFESSIONS OF AN INK-STAINED WRETCH

FOREWORD

"TELL HIM HIS POEM STINKS AND KICK HIM DOWN THE STAIRS."
– Walter Burns, the newspaper managing editor in *His Girl Friday*

"Do I look like a whore to you?"

That's what I've often wanted to say to innumerable marketing and public relations directors over the years, when they darken my office doorway to implore me to prostitute my editorial department's integrity to pursue their promotional goals.

Instead, to my eternal discredit, my actual response typically goes like this: "Glad to see you! Take a seat! How can I be of service?"

After this initial burst of hypocrisy, the two of us invariably commence an intricate *pas de deux*, in which I attempt to assist the marketer and at the same time preserve as much integrity as possible. Let's face facts: without sales dollars coming into the organization, all talk of editorial quality is moot. In today's global, hyperlinked, 24/7 economy, journalists can't afford to be prima donnas, living in ivory towers. Most journalists must master a delicate balancing act: they need to acquire and demonstrate marketing savvy, while simultaneously preserving editorial sanctity. The "church-state" separation between marketing and the press is no longer a wall — it's more akin to a permeable membrane. Welcome to journalism, the world's second oldest profession.

THE CONFESSIONS OF AN INK-STAINED WRETCH

Andrew Card, White House chief of staff for George W. Bush, explicitly acknowledged these facts of political life, when discussing the administration's plans to sell the American public on an invasion of Iraq. In September 2002, Card explained to *The New York Times*: "From a marketing point of view, you don't introduce new products in August." Of course, it also helps that these marketing-savvy GOP operatives possess a sharper taste for the jugular than their opponents, but I digress.

During the course of my long and varied career as a journalist, I have witnessed firsthand the most effective marketing methods from both sides of the church-state divide. I've learned ways to meld journalism with marketing because I've been forced to do it for more than two decades. The book you hold in your hands is a brutally frank, hands-on manual for manipulating the press. These pages will convey practical, real world advice on how to get the attention of working journalists, to promote your marketing/public relations message. I will deal with the everyday realities of the working press and how to make those realities work for you.

Each of my chapters will include "how to" checklists that are related to the themes of the respective chapter. It's as if a magician were violating his oath, by teaching you the tricks of the trade.

Wry jokes about "prostitution" aside, it is indeed possible to combine journalistic substance with marketing effectiveness; the two concepts are not mutually exclusive. You can help journalists maintain their integrity, and in the process make your marketing even more effective. Journalists and marketers alike can benefit from my experience in pulling off this balancing act. All it requires is a certain, um, moral flexibility. I'll show you how.

THE CONFESSIONS OF AN INK-STAINED WRETCH

> During the course of my long and varied career as a journalist, I have witnessed firsthand the most effective marketing methods from both sides of the church-state divide. I've learned ways to meld journalism with marketing because I've been forced to do it for more than two decades.

To be sure, I started my career with the highest idealism. Looking back on those salad days, in the late 1970s and early 1980s, it all seems rather quaint in retrospect. There was no Internet, no cell phones, not even word processors. I went through my entire college career with little more than a battle-scarred manual Royal typewriter and several hundred gallons of Liquid Paper. By today's high-tech standards, it seems as if I wrote my term papers by candlelight with a quill pen, to the background strains of harpsichord music.

I obtained a Master's Degree in English literature from Boston University, with the aim of becoming a professor. I have loved literature since I was a child and I wanted to convey this love to new generations of students. I envisioned myself in a tweed jacket, with patches on the elbows, wisely explicating the existentialist subtext in Herman Melville's *Moby Dick*. In the summers, I'd become an expatriate on the Left Bank, writing the Great American Novel while safely ensconced in a bistro by the Seine.

THE CONFESSIONS OF AN INK-STAINED WRETCH

My vision was a cliché and, thankfully, it never came to pass. Regardless, my experience in academia was profoundly disillusioning: I found it to be stultifying and downright boring. It was also during the era when Jacques Derrida and his gang of Gauloise-puffing deconstructionists were transforming the study of literature into a real bummer. As William Wordsworth put it, "We murder to dissect," and it certainly seemed that my joylessly analytical teachers were crucifying my favorite books until these texts' lifeblood was completed leached away.

To make matters worse, unbearably absurd academic politics raged behind the seemingly tranquil façades of the Back Bay brownstones that housed the graduate English department. This internecine professorial warfare made today's insurgency in Iraq seem tame by comparison. In the words of Dr. Henry Kissinger, erstwhile U.S. Secretary of State: "The reason politics in academia is so vicious is that the stakes are so small."

My less-than-happy stint in academia compelled me to pursue my old dream of becoming a journalist. I decided to get a second Master's Degree, in print journalism. Daily journalism, I felt, was the perfect melding of the active with the contemplative life. Again, it was a cliché, pursued by thousands of young saps like me, who were intoxicated by the romantic notion of investigative journalists taking on the system, as epitomized by Woodward and Bernstein.

However, even before *All The President's Men*, I had been brainwashed as a kid by corny black-and-white newspaper movies from the 1930s and 1940s. I envisioned my newspaper career as a wild, drunken ride in a Checker cab through noirish urban streets, banging out copy and knocking back whiskey with fast-talking dames like Rosalind Russell and tough guys in fedoras right out of Damon Runyon. The hordes of

www.inkstainedconfessions.com

THE CONFESSIONS OF AN INK-STAINED WRETCH

deluded (and soon-to-be-unemployed) kids with freshly minted journalism degrees proved that I wasn't alone in my delusions.

THE DARK AGES

Back in the Middles Ages, when I was starting out in this masochistic profession called journalism, I was a callow newspaperman burning with Pulitzer pretensions. One afternoon, the metro editor registered his impatience with one of my long-winded dispatches by slamming the Associated Press Stylebook on my desk.

"What are the three rules of good journalism?" he asked with weary disgust. Before I could stammer out an answer, he bellowed: "Focus, focus and focus!"

A quarter of a century later, I'm applying this timeless advice to everything I write. Readers today demand accurate, ahead-of-the-curve information. Suffering as a beat reporter taught me that the best way to gather this information is through personal contact with people in the field who are making things happen. This is a timeless rule that still applies, even in the age of Google and Yahoo.

That's why, despite the indignities of contemporary airline travel, it is obligatory for a journalist to apply shoe leather to the pavement on a regular basis. Preconceived notions are the bane of any profession, but they're especially harmful — even deadly — in a field such as journalism.

A.J. Liebling, the late, great editor and curmudgeon, put it this way: "There are three kinds of writers: The reporter, who writes what he sees; the interpretive reporter, who writes what he sees and what he construes to be its meaning; and the expert, who writes what he construes to be the meaning of what he hasn't seen."

THE CONFESSIONS OF AN INK-STAINED WRETCH

Good journalists know this; shrewd marketers know it, too. If you want to be a persuasive marketer, then you should know what constitutes good journalism. You should also know what constitutes bad journalism, which unfortunately is increasingly pushing out the good. Understand the mentality and needs of a journalist and you've got him, or her, in the palm of your hand. Trouble is, the vast majority of marketers haven't a clue about how the media really operates, and they're too incurious to learn.

I quickly learned — during my stints as a reporter on *The Lowell Sun, The Orlando Sentinel* and other newspapers — that the once noble pursuit of newspapering had changed from the days when Ben Hecht wrote his love letter, *The Front Page*, to his newspaper brethren. In our pragmatic corporate society, everything is turned into a commodity, and the news is no exception. Media consolidation has reduced the diversity and autonomy of news outlets in the country and put them under the thumb of marketers and accountants.

There was a time when the barons of media felt that they had a social obligation to inform the public. Today, they are driven by a fiduciary obligation to entertain consumers. The goal isn't excellent journalism; it's maximized shareholder returns. The result? Working in a newsroom today is about as much fun as working for an insurance company. Dumbing down the news, to appeal to the lowest common denominator, is the order of the day.

The advent of *USAToday* — McPaper — accelerated the trend toward shallow reporting that focuses more on Hollywood celebrities than on the inner workings of Congress. Designed as an eye-catching newspaper for ADD-afflicted people who typically don't read, the effect of Al Neuharth's brainchild has been permanent and far-reaching. Today, all journalism must entail lots of graphics and bullets and not too many

www.inkstainedconfessions.com

THE CONFESSIONS OF AN INK-STAINED WRETCH

> A.J. Liebling, the late, great editor and curmudgeon, put it this way: "There are three kinds of writers: The reporter, who writes what he sees; the interpretive reporter, who writes what he sees and what he construes to be its meaning; and the expert, who writes what he construes to be the meaning of what he hasn't seen."

words. Even the august *New Yorker* magazine runs much shorter articles these days. No one has the patience anymore to light an aromatic tobacco pipe and curl up with an earnest 12-part series on nuclear winter. All news must conform to the sensibilities of an instant gratification, hedonistic consumer society that gets most of its news and information from television. TV defines reality; nothing has really happened until it has appeared on the tube. Control television and you control society, just as surely as the computer jack in the back of Keanu Reeves's head in *The Matrix* controlled his perception of reality.

You only have a few seconds to grab your audience by the lapels; if your lede or first impression forces them to think, you've lost them.

No one is immune from these trends. Don't fight the wave — ride it out, like an opportunistic surfer. When the wave peters out, grab the next one.

THE CONFESSIONS OF AN INK-STAINED WRETCH

The magazine business is governed by the same relentless economic and social forces but occupies a more rarified atmosphere. While serving as a staff writer for *Inc.* magazine, I directly witnessed the glorious excesses of the go-go 1980s, when Zen Master Steve Jobs was inventing the personal computer market (and Silicon Valley's "Cult of Personality"), and "entrepreneur" was the hottest buzzword around. As a young magazine writer, I pursued my fantasies of being a swashbuckling Tom Wolfe on an expense account.

But even in the glitzy world of magazines, marketing realities trumped literary ambitions. Magazine publishers crave lists, rankings, industry round-ups — all sorts of gimmicks that generate advertising dollars. Similar to my days as a newspaperman, I often found myself creating magazine copy that would justify a preconceived advertising campaign. My assigning editors didn't resemble Ben Bradlee, as played by Jason Robards. They had more in common with Gordon Gekko. Some of my articles were predicated on very worthy topics, and I even managed to win an award or two, but too many of my stories were designed as ad bait.

But within all of these media trends lay enormous opportunities to sell your message. I'm writing this book to give marketers and public relations professionals the inside information on how to make these facts of life work for them. Despite these worrisome economic and social trends, one hopeful fact is emerging: markets are conversations. Markets consist of human individuals, not scientifically delineated demographic sectors. The essence of persuasion is to conduct conversations with members of the press in a human voice that seems natural and uncontrived. I will show you how to figuratively and literally speak in a voice that cuts through the cacophony and grabs a journalist's attention.

www.inkstainedconfessions.com

THE CONFESSIONS OF AN INK-STAINED WRETCH

As co-opted as they are, today's journalists remain a skeptical bunch, and that's a good thing. They're inundated all day with marketing and PR pitches and their email "in boxes" are clogged with unwanted spam. Slick marketing brochures, corporate mission statements and press releases — all of the fatuous collateral that speaks with a homogenized voice — come off as contrived and don't make a dent in their consciousness. The average American gawks at the lobotomy box (a.k.a., television) more than three hours a day. We're bombarded with a relentless barrage of commercials, from a variety of media, all vying for our attention. The white noise is deafening.

Therein lies a paradox. Within all of these discouraging trends, bright spots are emerging. The Internet and the "nichifying" of media are opening hitherto unavailable opportunities for marketers — and empowering individuals, to boot. Today's fiber-optically connected Global Village is returning us, in many ways, to the primal verities of the village, where communication was intimate and personalized — and a matter of survival. After all, the characteristic that distinguishes us from the rest of the animal kingdom is language. (Concurrently, if you debase language, you debase human beings.)

Corporations are trying to solidify their control of mass media, but at the same time, hyperlinks are subverting their control and dismantling hierarchies. Howard Beale, the suicidal has-been news anchor in *Network*, isn't the only one to shout: "I'm mad as hell, and I'm not taking it anymore!" Today, podcasters, bloggers and the rest of their ilk are proclaiming a similar rebellion and they're ushering in a new era of *perestroika* for the American press.

A PAIR OF DIMES = 20 CENTS

Marketers must exhibit guerrilla cunning to exploit this new paradigm; to influence an audience, they must engage in straight talk. (Did I just

THE CONFESSIONS OF AN INK-STAINED WRETCH

write the pretentious and overused term, "paradigm"? Sorry; it slipped out.) Anyway, if you still talk in the language of late 20th century marketing — the language of stilted and canned pitches — then you're talking to yourself. No one is listening.

The folks online aren't the same market who used to watch TV ads or read press releases. More than ever, markets are networks of individuals who speak among themselves. Your best means of persuading these individuals is to join their community and speak with a human voice.

As a journalist, nothing annoys me more than receiving unsolicited and generic email blasts, or phony-sounding press releases that were sent to thousands of other unwilling recipients. It also raises my ire, and makes me predisposed to work against you, if you call me and make a pitch that shows a complete lack of understanding regarding my publication's focus, my organizational role and my audience. The shotgun approach to marketing, by which a general message is sent to the amorphous hordes, is a guarantee of failure. Another note: misspell an editor's name or publication and your message is DOA. I'm always amazed at the propensity of most marketers for typographical error.

For the purposes of influencing the press, you must know how the Fourth Estate functions in the trenches, through the eyes of a journalist. Michael Corleone put it best, during a tête-à-tête with his consigliere, Tom Hagen: "One thing pop taught me, is to see things the way others see them. Now on that basis, anything is possible." It was this gangster ethos that helped me influence the press, during my stint as a press secretary in Congress.

There's a dirty little secret about the press that I'll reveal right now: they're mostly lazy bastards. If you make their job easier for them — promptly return their phone calls; spoon-feed them research; provide

THE CONFESSIONS OF AN INK-STAINED WRETCH

them the quotes they need to buttress their preconceived thesis — then you will exert considerable influence over the direction of their stories. To be sure, the term "working press" is often an oxymoron.

You must do your homework and tailor your message to the specific realities of your recipient. Do you hate it when telemarketers call your house? Journalists feel the same homicidal rage when a marketing or PR person calls them, making a pitch. "Get to know me!" Jon Lovitz would declare as a catchphrase, on a recurring *Saturday Night Live* sketch. The same applies to journalists; get to know them. Establish a relationship with them; cultivate them; buy them lunch; send them useful information. Don't just contact them when you need something. If a journalist's wife has a baby, send flowers to the hospital. If a journalist's parent dies, send flowers to the funeral. Make your interactions with them a two-way street. If you can't give them something of genuine utility, at least be interesting, for cryin' out loud.

But don't kid yourself: speaking with a genuine voice isn't a cute little trick. A personal relationship based on trust and mutual interests, not another hackneyed press release, gets the attention of journalists.

YOUR PRESS RELEASE SUCKS

I'll let you in on a harsh fact of journalistic life: A recent survey of editors found that less than 25 percent of the news releases they receive get used. Is this because the nation's newsgatherers already possess too many great ideas? Of course not. It's because most press releases are ineffectual. In this book, I will show you how to create and market press releases that don't suck. I'll also show you how to create a multimedia marketing message that uses all of the online tools available today, such as webcasts and podcasts. Your goal should be to marry old-school techniques with new ones.

THE CONFESSIONS OF AN INK-STAINED WRETCH

One of the most satisfying aspects of writing a book like this is my freedom to shun infotainment. Nonetheless, informative editorial doesn't have to be boring. Conveying information in an enjoyable format is not incompatible with serious, substantive journalism. I've interspersed this book with many colorful anecdotes from my own career, to add a human dimension to my assertions. Some personal anecdotes (especially those involving, say, my arrest record as a youth) have been left out. But otherwise, this book is an unvarnished and completely candid look at my life as an ink-stained wretch.

Scores of different media compete for the public's attention. Part of any editor's job is to cut through the cacophony and stand out from the crowd. The typical reader has an attention span of a gnat. In today's moronized culture of MTV, Jerry Springer and Matt Drudge, a publication must provide compelling writing and artwork — or get ignored.

The same holds true for your marketing message. Enough trees have died in vain, simply to create boring press releases that become snot rags. It's time to shed your self-absorption and join the fray. A journalist's life is a daily, tortuous hell of deadlines and the insatiable demands of the news hole. He or she must crank out sufficient copy, day in and day out, whether a story is warranted or not. You must understand the pressures of this world, to better leverage them to your advantage.

That's where this book comes in. My fellow ink-stained wretches of the press can quickly sense marketing bullshit, and when they do, little steel doors immediately snap shut in their minds. I'll show you how to pry open those doors, by demonstrating how to craft your message for maximum impact, and convey it in a more authentic voice.

George Burns put it best: "Sincerity! Once you can fake that, you've got it made."

www.inkstainedconfessions.com

Chapter 1
THE MEDIA BORG

How Six Giant Corporations Control
What You See, Hear and Read

Do you know who owns the media in your town? Chances are, the owners are a small, clubby group of highly paid executives who live far away in a gated community.

> **"RESISTANCE IS FUTILE."**
> – The Queen Borg, in
> *Star Trek: First Contact*

These managers may not know the needs of your community, but don't worry: they recognize each other on the golf course.

For the most part, they're likeminded and they share the same values. Their kids attend the same prep schools and their wives play tennis at the same country clubs. Sure, some of these executives are women, but most of them are white, middle-aged males.

If you think media consolidation is pernicious for democracy and you want to "fight the man," then run for office or petition the Federal Communications Commission. But if you're focused on making these profound changes work for you, then read this chapter. I'll explain the

THE CONFESSIONS OF AN INK-STAINED WRETCH

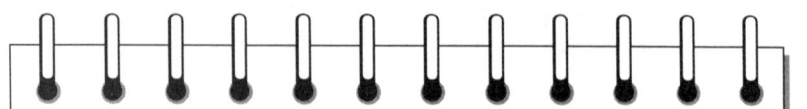

> Thomas Jefferson once said: "Were it left to me to decide whether we should have government without newspapers, or newspapers without government, I should not hesitate a moment to prefer the latter."

need to pursue an integrated approach to your message. I'll pinpoint the gatekeepers, each step of the way, and convey step-by-step advice on how to reach and influence them.

But first, you need to know the score. As they said during Watergate: follow the money. Despite a multitude of separate brand names emblazoned within colorful logos, most Americans would be shocked to know how little media choice actually exists. Media consolidation continues apace: in 1980 about 50 corporations controlled America's mass media. That was small enough. But since the dawn of the Reagan Era, a continual relaxation of FCC rules has fueled a relentless pace of mergers and acquisitions. Today, six multi-billion dollar behemoths dictate the vast majority of what you see, hear and read:
» AOL Time Warner
» Disney
» Viacom
» General Electric
» News Corp.
» Vivendi Universal

The old lines dividing various media have blurred; all types of media now form a vast interconnected and cross-owned international "media borg."

CHAPTER 1: THE MEDIA BORG

To get a perspective of what each of these multi-billion dollar media behemoths own, take a gander at the chart:

EYE-TO-EYE WITH THE BORG

AOL TIME WARNER	DISNEY	VIACOM	GENERAL ELECTRIC	NEWS CORP.	VIVENDI UNIVERSAL
Movies					
Warner Brothers	Walt Disney Pictures	Paramount	Universal Studios	20th Century Fox	Universal Studios
HBO	Touchstone	Showtime		Fox Searchlight	
New Line Cinema	Miramax	United Int'l Pictures			
		Famous Players			
Television					
WB	ABC	CBS	NBC (80%)	FOX	NBC (20%)
HBO	Disney Channel	MTV	CNBC (80%)	FX	CNBC (20%)
Cinemax	ESPN	Nickelodeon	MSNBC (80%)	FOX News	MSNBC (20%)
CNN	Soapnet	TV Land	Telemundo	FOX Movie Channel	
TNT		TNN	PAX	SKY	
TBS		BET	Bravo	National Geographic	
TCM		UPN	USA		
Cartoon Network		VH1	SciFi		
			Universal TV (80%)		Universal TV (20%)

www.inkstainedconfessions.com

THE CONFESSIONS OF AN INK-STAINED WRETCH

AOL TIME WARNER	DISNEY	VIACOM	GENERAL ELECTRIC	NEWS CORP.	VIVENDI UNIVERSAL
Publishing					
Time Magazine	Hyperion	Simon and Schuster		HarperCollins	Houghton Mifflin
People				New York Post	Vivendi Universal
TimeLife				Times of London	
Sports Illustrated					
Music					
Warner Bro Records	Hollywood Records			Festival	Universal Music Group
Atlantic	Mammoth Records				Polygram
Elektra	Buena Vista Records				Geffen Records
Rhino					A&M
					Island
					Decca
					Deutshe Gramophone
					Verve
					Motown
					MCA

CHAPTER 1: THE MEDIA BORG

AOL TIME WARNER	DISNEY	VIACOM	GENERAL ELECTRIC	NEWS CORP.	VIVENDI UNIVERSAL
Other					
	Disney Theme Parks	Blockbuster Video	Madison Square Garden	Knicks	
	ABC Radio	CBS Radio	Knicks	Liberty	
	ESPN Radio	Paramount Theme Park	Liberty	Rangers	
	Mighty Ducks		Rangers	L.A. Dodgers	
	Anaheim Angels			Staples Center	
	Disney Stores				

Source: publicly available records

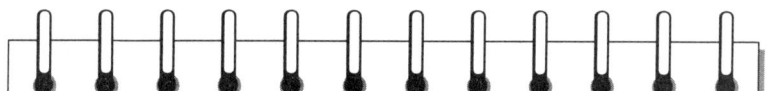

> Reporters learn self-censorship, they internalize the values of their organization and they instinctively know which stories will get positive feedback (and promotions and raises) from their supervisors, and which won't. No one has to overtly tell them what to report and write; the agenda of allowable stories is unspoken and understood.

www.inkstainedconfessions.com

THE CONFESSIONS OF AN INK-STAINED WRETCH

Thomas Jefferson once said: "Were it left to me to decide whether we should have government without newspapers, or newspapers without government, I should not hesitate a moment to prefer the latter."

Mr. Jefferson would be dismayed by the dwindling alternatives. Today, 10 companies own newspapers that distribute more than 51 percent of the nation's weekday circulation. Take a look at this chart:

NUMBER OF DAILY NEWSPAPERS OWNED BY THE LARGEST CHAINS

Gannett	91	Knight Ridder *	32
Tribune Co.	12	Advance	26
N.Y. Times Co.	17	Dow Jones	16
Hearst	12	MediaNews	43
McClatchy*	11	Scripps	22
Cox Newspapers	17	Freedom Comm.	28
Lee Enterprises	38	CNHI	107
Belo	4	Media General	25
Washington Post Co.	2	Hollinger	7
Morris Comm.	27	Copley	9
Pulitzer	14	Journal Register Co.	22

* McClatchy agreed to buy Knight Ridder's newspapers in March 2006. At press time, regulators were reviewing McClatchy's plans to sell off 12 of the newspapers; the continued existence of these newspapers is in doubt.

Source: *publicly available records.*

These statistics tell you to forget the myth of a "liberal" press. To be sure, most individual reporters may lean leftward, because the sort of person who chooses a relatively low-paying profession such as journalism has a liberal arts temperament that translates into a liberal, philosophical attitude towards life. But don't kid yourself: journalism's ink-

CHAPTER 1: THE MEDIA BORG

stained wretches get their paychecks from the conservative Republican businessmen who own and control these huge media corporations.

Reporters learn self-censorship, they internalize the values of their organization and they instinctively know which stories will get positive feedback (and promotions and raises) from their supervisors, and which won't. No one has to overtly tell them what to report and write; the agenda of allowable stories is unspoken and understood.

So you can see there's a lot more to reporting than just telling the reader what happened, who did it and when, where and why it happened (and why it matters) — the holy "Five Ws" taught in Journalism 101 courses throughout the land.

Case in point: General Electric is a major defense contractor and builder of nuclear energy equipment. Look at the chart of GE's television holdings and you'll understand why you'll never see NBC's Brian Williams introduce a story about wasteful defense spending or nuclear power plant safety.

Even Brenda Starr, the dame reporter in the famous comic strip, recently lamented: "Sometimes I think newspapers care more about profits than they do about people."

But here's the good news, dear reader: other media voices are emerging that are outside of the control of the major media monoliths. They are smaller, localized, personal, intimate and fiercely independent. They're the voices of bloggers, webcasters, podcasters and other players who are embracing the disruptive technologies of the New Media. As I will show in successive chapters, these voices convey an ameliorative diversity to the public discussion. They are usurping the officially sanctioned and intellectually sterile talking points foisted on society by Big Brother.

www.inkstainedconfessions.com

THE CONFESSIONS OF AN INK-STAINED WRETCH

THE GATEKEEPER WEARS FISHNET STOCKINGS

The advent of the Media Borg means that the barriers to entry for getting press play have been lowered. The media's increasing interconnectedness is accelerated and amplified by the advent of the Internet. With the Internet, it also makes it easier to *bypass* the former barriers to entry. A grizzled, tough-minded editor with decades of experience rarely stands in your way anymore. It's now astonishingly easy to insert information — often, bad information — into the media "conversation." The gatekeeper is not only easier to access, but if she knows you, she'll readily invite you home for the night.

Consider the rise of the conservative establishment and how it works in the real world. A Republican operative wants to smear a candidate; he feeds dirt about the candidate's personal life (real or fabricated) to Matt Drudge, who dutifully puts it on his web site. Then, Rupert Murdoch's empire of press and opinion — Fox News, *New York Post, Weekly Standard* — gives the story "legs" by covering it. The rest of the media is forced to cover the manufactured event and — voila! — the virus has entered the bloodstream of the media, courtesy of the Drudge Report.

Another scenario: Republican operatives make sure that a negative book about an opponent gets published by a right-wing publishing company (Regnery, for example); the book (typically rife with shoddy or fabricated research) becomes an artificial "bestseller" because conservative book clubs quickly buy up bulk copies; the author is interviewed on Fox; his thesis becomes "news."

A perfect example of this marketing tactic is reflected by the "Swift Boat Veterans for Truth" smear orchestrated by the Bush campaign against U.S. Senator John Kerry during the 2004 presidential election. I visited the Regnery offices recently, and on the wall in the lobby I saw the cover of the Swift Boat "book" posted next to a newspaper headline

CHAPTER 1: THE MEDIA BORG

that read "Bush Defeats Kerry." These editors think like political operatives because that's what they are.

The greatest marketer in American life today is Karl Rove. As Rove commented about the Vietnam War hero Kerry, shortly after Kerry was nominated as the Democratic candidate for president: "When we're done with him, people won't be sure which side he fought on."

Indeed, let's examine the competing Vietnam War records: George W. Bush was in the Texas Air National Guard. John Kerry, meanwhile, went to 'Nam and won three Purple Hearts, a Silver Star and a Bronze Star. But which man ended up on the defensive, concerning his war record? It was Kerry. The triumph of marketing!

Let me hasten to add, I've emphasized Republican tactics because of my grudging admiration for the GOP's effectiveness as marketers. The Democrats can make no claims to moral or political superiority. Democratic successes can be just as ruthless, but they're fewer in number (e.g., the personal destruction of Robert Bork and the creation of a new political term, "to bork"). The Democrats would follow the Grand Old Party's example, if they were only competent enough. When observing the invariable missteps of Democrats and the pathetic weaknesses of their political marketing, it's like watching my beloved Red Sox blow an early lead. I want to cry out: "Can't anybody here play this game?"

Regardless of your party affiliation or ideological persuasion, the lesson remains the same: media convergence means the death of reality. As a Bush operative dismissively told a print reporter: "You guys are reality based." Or as Bill Clinton once said: "It depends on what the meaning of the word 'is' is."

www.inkstainedconfessions.com

THE CONFESSIONS OF AN INK-STAINED WRETCH

SHOW ME THE MONEY
EIGHT STEPS FOR THINKING LIKE THE BORG

When crafting any media message, regardless of the medium, consider these overarching rules. These rules supplement other writing rules mentioned throughout this book:

1. Always consider the money angle. Few subjects are as interesting and pervasive as money. When considering the crux of your message, stop to ask yourself: How does this translate into dollars and cents? How does it affect business profits and jobs? Who stands to financially gain, and why? Even if your subject ostensibly has nothing to do with money, if you think a little deeper, you'll discover that it really does.

2. Emphasize the local. The money angle is most compelling when it's translated into local jobs or profits for local companies. If you're touting a corporate merger, focus on the ramifications for local employment and economic development.

3. Get your terms right. The money angle in press releases and other marketing collateral is often undermined by jargon, poor arithmetic or sheer ignorance of financial and business basics. Even if the targeted journalist appears to be savvy about subjects related to money and finances, approach your subject from the perspective of a person who is reading about business for the first time. Don't rely on a lot of fancy financial gobbledygook. Next to your AP Stylebook, keep handy a copy of Barron's "Dictionary of Finance and Investment Terms."

CHAPTER 1: THE MEDIA BORG

4. **Get your math right.** To highlight a notable example, it's astounding to me how often reporters screw up "percent" and "percentage point." For example, five percent is not five percentage points. To cite a specific usage: A presidential approval rating of 50 percent is 5 percentage points, not five percent, greater than 45 percent approval.

5. **Broaden your appeal.** As you localize, simultaneously broaden the appeal of your pitch. Editors look for stories that make readers identify and empathize. They want readers to say something like: "Oh yeah, my Uncle Eddie went through that." Draw a line from the macro (e.g., mergers and acquisitions and inflation statistics) to the micro (jobs, paychecks and personal triumphs over economic adversity). Tell the story behind the statistics.

6. **Lionize local entrepreneurs.** I've lost count of the profiles I've written about local business heroes. Readers love them; assignment editors love them even more. We live in the age of *People* magazine and "Entertainment Tonight." You must personalize your pitch as much as possible. The Horatio Alger rags-to-riches formula still plucks the old heartstrings.

7. **Use language that's evocative of money.** Get in the habit of using phrases such as "pocketbook," or "wallet." They may seem trite to you, but they grab the attention of editors. Instead of a headline that says: "Health Provider Costs Rise," consider punchier language, such as: "Hospital Costs Clobber Patients' Wallets." (See box, "Medical Economics 101," page 34.)

THE CONFESSIONS OF AN INK-STAINED WRETCH

8. **Spotlight recognizable brands and names.** Brands are the coin of the realm. Companies nurture and protect their brands, as surely as a lion protects her cubs. Brands get people's attention, which means they get journalists' attention, too. Be a namedropper.

Real world case in point: while a reporter on *The Orlando Sentinel*, I covered the Tylenol tampering scare. It was a great chance for me to get front-page stories in the paper, because Tylenol is a ubiquitous brand. Of course, it says something about the morally debased nature of journalists when they view human tragedy as a chance to get on the front page, but as Walter Cronkite used to say, that's the way it is. When I worked at *The Sentinel*, I woke up every morning with a fire in the belly, wondering how on earth I could get a story on Page A1 that day (see my Tylenol and Contac stories, page 33).

THEY MIGHT BE GIANTS

Luce. Paley. Hearst. Pulitzer. There was a time when a media empire was driven by the passion of a solitary individual. These individuals were visionaries who exerted iron-fisted control over their companies. Sure, they were capitalists, but their primary goal wasn't making money for its own sake. Instead, their strongest motivation was to communicate and affect society. Their competitors — the guys they wanted to beat and impress — were fellow dreamers who shared the same ethos. William Randolph Hearst, who will always be remembered through the unflattering prism of Orson Welles' Charles Foster Kane, was indeed a yellow journalist. But at least he was a mensch. He was driven by the need for power, recognition and status. His goals transcended mere money.

Say what you want about the early corporate giants, at least they built things. They made profits, but in the process they propelled innovation and raised everyone's standard of living. The media pioneers who put

CHAPTER 1: THE MEDIA BORG

Contac shares sales lead in tampering-crisis rebound

By John F. Persinos
OF THE SENTINEL STAFF

Contac, left out in the cold when it was taken off store shelves last March, has shaken off the ill effects of an Orlando tampering incident and returned healthier than ever.

The non-prescription cold and allergy remedy, manufactured by SmithKline Beckman Corp. of Philadelphia, has recouped all the market share it lost after product-tampering episodes that drew nationwide attention.

"Contac has more than recovered," said Jeremy Heymsfeld, spokesman for SmithKline. "It's now No. 1."

But it has not come without huge cost. The company has spent $40 million on advertising since reintroducing the product in August. Industry officials estimate total sales of Contac at only $60 million in 1985.

Still, the medication's ability to regain public acceptance is considered a major victory in crisis management, reminiscent of Johnson & Johnson's efforts after two tampering incidents involving the pain-reliever Tylenol.

"Both SmithKline and Johnson

Please see CONTAC, A-6

Reprinted by permission of The Orlando Sentinel [5/12/86].

Drug makers continue war a

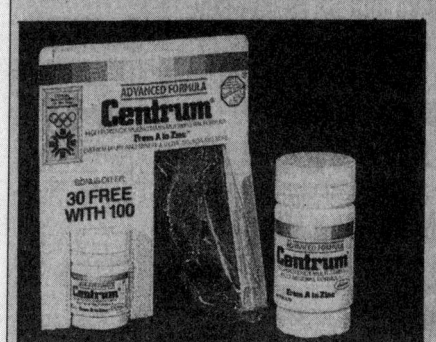

By John F. Persinos
OF THE SENTINEL STAFF

Despite the flurry of headlines about the vulnerability of over-the-counter drug capsules, industry analysts say that efforts to make capsules safer will not significantly increase their cost.

Nearly all drug companies have chosen tamper-resistant packaging — rather than new forms of medication — as an antidote for the drug-tampering scourge stretching from Orlando to Seattle.

Reprinted by permission of The Orlando Sentinel [5/18/86].

www.inkstainedconfessions.com

THE CONFESSIONS OF AN INK-STAINED WRETCH

MEDICAL ECONOMICS

When I was editor of medical newsletters at St. Anthony's Publishing, I was strongly swayed by arguments that brought stories down to dollars and cents for our readers, who were administrators in doctor's offices. For example: an analyst with a health care consultancy pitched me a story predicated on Medicare claims review. Boring, right? Not the way he pitched it. He used hot button language that got my attention — and got his story ink. I remember him saying to me on the phone: "Claims adjusters in the Medicare program are gonna cost your readers a bundle." When I heard that phrase, I sat up, took notice, and started taking notes. Here are the first two paragraphs of the story that I eventually wrote, as it appeared on the front page of the newsletter:

St. Anthony's Payment Upd[ate]

Reimbursement issues and answers for the practicing physician

Volume 1, Number 1
March 1990

Inside this Issue ...
Unbundled Claims Under Scrutiny 1
PRO Review of Physician Records Is Imminent 2
Documentation Increasingly Linked to Payment 3
Reimbursement Questions and Answers ... 4
Guidelines for Faxing Attestations Available 4

Published by
St. Anthony Publishing, Inc.

Crackdown on Unbundling Can Cost You a Bundle

There's a new breed of claims police afoot that physicians shouldn't take lightly. Third-party payers are using new computer software to thwart "unbundling," the increasingly prevalent practice of coding a single operative session as a number of separate incidental or diagnostic procedures.

At best, unbundling is an honest mistake; at worst, it's fraud. Either way, getting blamed for unbundling increasingly means reduced or delayed payment, and, if physicians continue the practice, a very unsavory reputation.

There are steps physicians should take now to protect themselves

To better prepare them[selves], [physi]cians also should take [note of] how unbundling softw[are and] what types of treatmen[t] are likely to be flagge[d].

Like most unbundling [software], GMIS's product, calle[d...,] reviews claims against coding rules and logic[al] codes. The software o[ffers rec]ommendations, leavin[g final] decisions to the insure[r. In some] cases, though, the insu[rer's] recommendations.

The following are act[ual] procedures that were f[...]

Reprinted by permission of Ingenix, Inc.

CHAPTER 1: THE MEDIA BORG

their names on companies were self-made men. Their egos were large, but so were their legacies to society. They built libraries, created awards and founded schools. Today's media baron philanthropists are Lilliputians by comparison.

As a result of ruthless globalization, consolidation and commercialization, finance men in yellow ties and gray flannel suits increasingly run media companies. This new type of media leader casts his eyes to Wall Street, not the public's right to know.

You won't find this managerial elite poring over editorial copy in the newsroom. They're too busy writing memos, launching leveraged buy-outs, hoarding stock options and "right-sizing" the rank-and-file (after someone decided that "down-sizing" wasn't euphemistic enough). When AOL merged with Time-Warner, there was a lot of hyperbolic talk of synergy. Recent history has shown that the word "synergy" is a euphemism for layoffs.

Media corporations manufacture consensus. Throughout history, those in authority have always known that to control the public, they must control information. Media corporations are interlocked in common financial interest with other huge industries and with a handful of international banks. Look at the names on the boards of directors of Fortune 500 companies; many of the same names will show up on the boards of media companies.

Don't misunderstand me: I'm not positing a paranoid conspiracy theory. These trends are not the result of conscious machinations, perpetrated by a secret society of men in frock coats who meet in the basement of the Harvard Club. Media consolidation is not the purposeful strategy of the Trilateral Commission or the Business Roundtable or the Elders of Zion. The rise of the multinational corporation has been an inexorable economic trend since John D. Rockefeller and the

THE CONFESSIONS OF AN INK-STAINED WRETCH

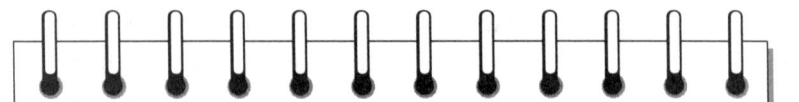

> A Republican operative wants to smear a candidate; he feeds dirt about the candidate's personal life to Matt Drudge, who puts it on his web site. Then, Rupert Murdoch's empire of press and opinion gives the story "legs" by covering it. The rest of the media is forced to cover the manufactured event and – voila! – the virus has entered the media bloodstream.

Gilded Age. Few entities can marshal resources as efficiently as the large global corporation; its emergence as a dominant force was unstoppable. The real issue is, how can society democratize corporations and make them more accountable to social needs? How can we humanize the face of global capitalism? That's a question for another time, and perhaps another book.

For the purposes of *this* book, it's enough for you to know that the lack of a conspiracy does not mean that huge media corporations lack clout and neglect to use it in a coordinated way. These organizations share the same values and they mold American public opinion accordingly.

THE MOOLAH IS THE MESSAGE

What does all this mean for you, the marketer? You must always remain mindful of the ethos that drives today's media corporation. These organizations maximize profit by keeping stories simple, to appeal to the lowest common denominator.

CHAPTER 1: THE MEDIA BORG

Also recognize the simplistic prism through which editors look at stories. Political coverage emphasizes personalities and the horse race, at the expense of in-depth public policy analysis. Business coverage emphasizes easily understood consumer stories, personal finance advice, lionizing portraits of CEOs and the ups and downs of Wall Street. Environmental reporting is given short shrift; labor reporting is almost non-existent. The moolah is the message.

When I was a reporter at *The Orlando Sentinel* in the mid-1980s, a major part of my beat was health care. The story ideas that my editors liked and approved tended to revolve around managed care and the need for medical cost containment. I wrote scores of articles about Health Maintenance Organizations (HMOs), typically portraying them as a wonderful innovation that was helping tame the health inflation beast. In story meetings with editors, a press release titled "Hospital Union Strikes over Low Pay" would immediately get tossed in the trash, or at best the story would be relegated to a single-paragraph "news brief."

However, a press release titled "HMOs Report New Gains Against Out-of-Control Health Costs" would immediately get assigned. If you looked closer, you'd probably discover that the credible-sounding statistics larded throughout the press release originally came from the HMOs themselves. Throughout the 1980s, I witnessed firsthand how managed care companies skewed journalistic coverage in their favor, by portraying themselves as fiscally responsible guardians of health delivery.

History has since taught us otherwise and managed care is now held in extremely low regard by both the public and the medical profession, in large part because of the strong-arm tactics of HMOs and similar entities that deny access to health care. The $900 billion-a-year health care-industrial complex accounts for 14 percent of gross domes-

THE CONFESSIONS OF AN INK-STAINED WRETCH

tic product in the U.S. It's ruled by HMOs, for-profit hospital chains, insurance companies, pharmaceutical manufacturers and legions of Gucci-clad lobbyists.

Marcus Welby is dead. The kindly, silver-haired physician in a white lab coat is no longer the gatekeeper to the health care system. Managed care plans — and their ruthless fixation on the bottom line — now dominate medicine. But for many years after their inception, managed care corporations were showered with fulsome publicity, a testament to the clever manner in which they promoted themselves as brave slayers of the inflationary dragon.

The lesson? If you want assignment editors to pay attention to your press release, you must think like the Borg (see sidebar, page 30).

Again, don't misunderstand me: I'm a fervent capitalist as well. To borrow from Winston Churchill's phrase about democracy, capitalism is the worst economic system — except for all the others. In fact, my appreciation of capitalism is so strong, I wholeheartedly urge you to buy as many copies of this book as possible (my daughter's college tuition is very expensive!).

But I'm also a realist. To maximize your effectiveness as a marketer, you must deal with things not as you wish them, but as they really are. Media managers aren't intellectuals. They're not poets and they're not philosophers. They're businesspeople. They have mortgages to pay and kids to send through college. They won't embrace anything that will jeopardize their cushy white-collar jobs. Don't give them stories you think they should run. Give them exactly what they want — and give it to 'em good and hard.

CHAPTER 1: THE MEDIA BORG

Most cities are one-newspaper towns. Big media publishers are like feudal lords who have won civil wars in medieval times. They preside over their domains with a disdain for competition or anyone who can be perceived as an interloper. They behave as if they rule by divine right. However, as I will explain, their media fiefdoms are under attack. As typically happens with powerful elites, they've gotten complacent and their hubris is coming back to haunt them. Web-based media, in all of its pragmatic anarchy, is threatening the ramparts.

The following chapters will spell out specific "how to" steps for waging a successful marketing guerrilla campaign that exploits the realities — and the weaknesses — of the media elite. By taking a blended approach, and combining conventional with innovative approaches, you can generate maximum publicity with minimum investment. In our next chapter, you'll see how to make all this media consolidation work to your advantage.

Chapter 2

SWEETHEART, GET ME REWRITE

How to Push the Media's "Hot Buttons"

You have a message and you want The Borg to carry it for you. How do you get into the belly of the beast?

First, change your thinking. It's no longer about television, newspapers or magazines. Remember, the old lines dividing the media are blurred. Those media are the means to an end, not the ends in themselves. Your goal is to create an infectious word-of-mouth that spreads through The Borg like a virus. As I said in my Foreword, markets are conversations. Your goal should be to take an action that serves as a catalyst for a conversation, and then supplement that conversation as it travels.

> "NO ONE BUT A BLOCKHEAD EVER WROTE BUT FOR MONEY."
> – Dr. Samuel Johnson

THE CONFESSIONS OF AN INK-STAINED WRETCH

```
Establish a human relationship with
reporters. Call them when you
don't necessarily need something at
the moment, while fully realizing that
you will need something in the near
future. Take them to lunch, and always
pick up the tab — always!
```

The best way to initiate a conversation is to appeal to basic instincts. In Chapter Three, I emphasize the basic structural and stylistic rules of creating content. Here, I focus on the proper themes for your message, and how to successfully couple your message with media outreach.

In a press release, phone call or marketing collateral, you need to push "hot buttons" right from the start. Here's a list to always keep in mind, regardless of the focus on your message:

THE TOP SEVEN MESSAGE DRIVERS
1. Sex
2. Taboos
3. Celebrities
4. Humor
5. Oddities
6. Inside information/secrets
7. Sentimentality

Sex tops the list, as it often does. It's always good to get celebrities somehow wrapped up in your message, as well. Our culture worships

CHAPTER 2: SWEETHEART, GET ME REWRITE

celebrities; Hollywood is the new Valhalla. There was a time when a celebrity was known for his or her achievements; now, someone is a celebrity merely for being famous.

That's why more Americans can identify Paris Hilton than, say, their own congressman. Very few Americans can name the CEO of Viacom, the multi-billionaire Sumner Redstone, an octogenarian who wields enormous power over all of our lives. But hey, we all know about Jennifer Aniston and almost every detail of her personal life. (Granted, Jennifer looks a heck of a lot better in a bathing suit.)

Make sure your message incorporates at least one of the seven drivers; the more you can credibly include, the better. The inclusion of at least one driver guarantees that you'll start a conversation — first, between yourself and the reporter/writer; then, between the reporter/writer and the assigning editor; and finally, among the decision-making editors who sit in story meetings where they hash out what the respective publication will cover.

HOW DOES IT WORK IN PRACTICE?

I'll cite a specific example from my career. While a cub reporter at *The Lowell Sun*, I covered town meetings. The towns I covered thought they were sleepy, contented little burgs where everyone got along — until this reporter came to town. These good citizens had no idea that their neighborhoods were cauldrons of strife, until I was civic minded enough to point it out to them.

I remember covering one meeting in particular, in which the local school board discussed curriculum changes. It was interminable and boring, and I was about to despair that I would ever get a playable story out of the proceedings, until the agenda turned to...sex education. When I heard a school board member utter the word "sex," I

THE CONFESSIONS OF AN INK-STAINED WRETCH

immediately stopped doodling in my notebook and sat up in my chair, like a pointer on the hunt.

I could have covered weightier matters — the school budget, major facility construction projects, teacher pension plans, etc. But my editor would not have run those stories; when I got back to the newsroom, my efforts would have sparked what's known in journalistic circles as the dreaded MEGO syndrome (My Eyes Glaze Over). I never would have gotten my byline in the paper the next day if I focused on the school board's arcane administrative deliberations.

That's why I filed a story on sex education. Here's the lede that ran on the first page of *The Sun* — above the fold, baby — the next morning. (For the complete article, go to www.inkstainedconfessions.com.)

Fifth graders may ... education film th...

By JOHN F. PERSINOS
Sun Staff

WESTFORD – Fifth grade boys and girls who receive parental permission will see a film on menstruation this fall – in separate rooms with a school nurse present.

The school board last night unanimously supported the recommendation of Superintendent Everard Nicholson to offer the informational film.

"We should have the film back in the fifth grade, for the health aspect," he said, "but we should have the nurses show it. Take it out of teachers' hands, and put it in the hands of ...

Nicholson opinion that t... ly, to avoid e... with nurses to... the boys are s... are usually a...

He said, "... together, they... them separate... will be produ...

To avoid p... Nicholson s... approval be o... to a student.

Reprinted by permission of The Lowell Sun [8/10/82].

CHAPTER 2: SWEETHEART, GET ME REWRITE

In the quiet suburban town of Westford, my story qualified for what *Washington Post* editor Ben Bradlee used to refer to as "holy shit!" journalism. A lot of parents had their breakfasts spoiled that morning, as soon as they picked up their *Lowell Sun* and glanced at the front page. ("Whoa, Mabel! Did you read this? They're gonna show our little Suzie a movie about menstruation!")

Yellow journalism? In the words of Bugs Bunny: "Hmmmm, could be!" But the story was accurate, it was true, and hey, it made me a minor celebrity in Westford. When I stumbled upon sex education in Westford, way back in the summer of 1982, I was able to milk the topic in the following weeks for several prominently placed stories. It is no exaggeration to say that Sex Ed launched my career.

As a marketer and PR professional, you must view your promotional needs through the same prism. Don't sensationalize your message in an obvious, ham-handed way. If you get too cheesy, it will backfire on you. What you need to do is find a way to accurately and credibly emphasize at least one of the seven "drivers" in your press outreach. Never make something up; if the press ever catches you in a lie, you're dead (unless you work at the White House, in which case, you can seemingly lie with impunity). Simply flesh out and bring to the fore the driver(s) that inherently exist in your message.

That said, the sensibilities of tabloid journalism dominate all journalism today. While circulation for news-related publications continues its inexorable decline, the circulation numbers for celebrity magazines continue to soar. Most news is reduced to easily grasped melodramatic stories, with heroes and bad guys. Even more disturbing is the melding of fantasy with reality. Many Americans have a tough time distinguishing between an action movie and a newscast; it all sort of blurs in their mind while they channel surf. It's no surprise that TV newscasts often deploy the techniques of movies, or even of music videos.

THE CONFESSIONS OF AN INK-STAINED WRETCH

Entertainment, news, Hollywood, celebrities, politicians — nowadays, it's all the same damn thing. Two words sum up this convergence: "Governor Schwarzenegger."

This tabloid dynamic is certainly true of television news, but it even affects the prestige print press. Sex, violence and mayhem are the biggest attention getters. There's an old saying in the newsroom: "If it bleeds, it leads." Hence, my front-page newspaper story on menstruation.

My list of "seven message drivers" directly exploits this situation. Gathering the news — and influencing the news gatherers — is a different exercise than gathering the truth. Society might be better off if journalists simply gave up all pretense to being objective establishers of truth and acknowledged that they are agents for other parties who wish to get certain information into the public realm. Behind every ostensibly objective news story, there is a "back story" of manipulation.

Sophisticated consumers of news are aware of this back story and they're able to read between the lines. They can detect a story's subtext and, perhaps, discern who influenced its behind-the-scenes creation. Luckily for marketers and PR professionals, the vast majority of news consumers are not sophisticated. They come to the news bowl with about as much discernment as a hungry canine digging into Dog Chow. Filling the bowl with your particular brand of chow requires outreach.

GETTING STARTED

Media outreach begins with homework. As Sun Tzu said: "The battle is won before the fight, through preparation." A constant source of irritation for journalists is the unwillingness of marketing folks to first conduct upfront research before contacting them. It reflects laziness and lack of respect. Determine who covers the beat you're occupying; even

CHAPTER 2: SWEETHEART, GET ME REWRITE

magazines assign writers certain beats. Then, determine that reporter's assigning editor.

You can get this information from the masthead. If the information isn't listed, skim the publication and determine who tends to cover politics, high technology, real estate, etc. If these identities aren't readily available, then call the managing editor and ask directly. The editor-in-chief rules the roost, but he's akin to a general in the military. His job is to shake hands, look impressive, bark a few vague commands and go to lunch. In the military, colonels wield the genuine power. In the newsroom or editorial department, real power is wielded by the managing editor. The ME has a finger in every pie; he or she makes the editorial trains run on time. The editor-in-chief worries about strategic issues and whether his tie matches his shirt; the ME runs operational aspects with an iron fist.

Establish a human relationship with reporters. Call them when you don't necessarily need something at the moment (while fully realizing that you will need something in the near future). Take them to lunch, and always pick up the tab — always! To break the ice with a reporter you've never met before, start small. It begins when mutual business needs have thrown you together. Escalate from there, with personal gestures.

If you make the commitment to wine and dine a journalist, don't cheap out at the last minute. A potential source once invited me to the most expensive restaurant in town, and I eagerly accepted. A week later he sent an invoice to my boss for the cost of the meal! My boss didn't pay it, but he did needle me about how the two of us ran up a tab of $279. Needless to say, that guy went on my shit list. (On the other hand, that second bottle of pinot noir was exquisite.)

THE CONFESSIONS OF AN INK-STAINED WRETCH

Schmooze with them; tell them dirty jokes; strike up a conversation about their favorite sports team; ask them about their kids. Don't be smarmy and obvious about it. Just make them a part of your Rolodex and your everyday network. Think of it as farming; you're sowing seeds for a future harvest. But don't go overboard with the manure.

Learn the reporter's beat; become conversant and knowledgeable about the areas he or she covers. Earn their respect by providing story ideas or insights that don't have strings attached. Make your relationship a two-way street. Also, get to know the chain-of-command in the reporter's office. Who's the boss? How do stories get approved?

Some years back I was covering the hazardous materials transportation beat — real glamorous, I know, but I had bills to pay. But since I was the only reporter in Washington who covered this beat full-time, the group that represents the hazmat haulers made my life a lot easier by showering me with fact sheets, comments from industry officials, etc. I'm not saying I slanted the coverage in their direction, but I couldn't avoid representing their point of view in my stories.

Reporters are under enormous daily pressure. If you understand their deadlines and their editorial needs, and you demonstrate ways in which you can make their lives easier, you will have a foot in the door. You will get an audience.

FOREPLAY REQUIRED

As a matter of course, the submission of all press releases and marketing collateral should be followed by personal contact (see page 52). Before contacting a member of the press, create a list of "talking points" for yourself to follow while you're on the phone. Weave in your sound bites, but deliver them in a spontaneous way. Keep in mind, this presentation only establishes the parameters for your discussion.

CHAPTER 2: SWEETHEART, GET ME REWRITE

Within these parameters, you will extemporize and strive for conversational spontaneity. Engage in plenty of ad-libbing. You want to create a lively give-and-take, rather than a scripted and stilted conversation. However, it's always important to first create a script to serve as a foundation and a "safety net."

Think of your script as sheet music for a jazz musician. You'll play the theme as written, but you'll also improvise and perform plenty of riffs. When first contacting a new reporter, your goal is feigned spontaneity. As you get to know the reporter, this spontaneity will become more genuine. When establishing relationships with the media, don't think in terms of days or weeks, or even months. Act as if you're creating a relationship that will last for decades. Chances are, it *will* last that long.

Cultivating the press is a 24/7 effort that never ceases. It's like going on a date: you first have to buy dinner and flowers, and make an effort at conversation, if you expect to score. Getting into a reporter's good graces is similar to pleasing a spouse: you must be a good listener. Otherwise, you'll never get into the reporter's pants (so to speak).

Help should be a two-way street. Provide information, tips, scoops, background research and contacts for the journalists you are seeking to influence. If the journalist works for a daily or weekly publication, ask to see a list of story ideas or assignments, with the suggestion that maybe you can help. Offer to introduce journalists to sources and make your Rolodex available.

Reporters are under enormous pressure to produce results. Most of the time, the boss is a sadist who's breathing down their neck, threatening physical violence if a deadline is missed. That's why reporters will grab any offer of help they can get. So don't worry: if you ask to see a story list, they probably won't be turf conscious. Any assistance that spares

THE CONFESSIONS OF AN INK-STAINED WRETCH

them humiliation in front of their peers — and which gets them to happy hour on time — will be appreciated.

If the journalist works for a magazine, ask to see a story calendar. You can also find these editorial calendars online, situated on the publication's web site. As a magazine editor, I've crafted — and been compelled to follow — editorial calendars that map out every issue for the next 12 months. For the most part, these stories are created to bring in advertising dollars.

Let's say the editorial calendar lists, for the June issue, a cover story called "The Latest Aerospace Engine Technology." This story is probably timed to coincide with a major engine trade show in or near the month of June. If the editor is a journalist with any sort of integrity or talent, then he or she dreads the June cover story, because it's a compulsory piece of "ad bait" that must be written to attract and please advertisers. In fact, the cover story is likely to be an evergreen topic that runs every June and, as such, is dry and boring and lacks real newsworthiness.

Every June, the editor must manufacture some sort of news hook to justify the cover story on aerospace engines — without this news hook appearing to be too contrived.

That's where you come in. You will ingratiate yourself, and influence coverage, if you call an editor, demonstrate knowledge of the editorial calendar and then suggest ways in which you can help the editor fulfill some of the journalistic obligations that are listed in the calendar. Make yourself available as a *de facto* staffer who will handle some of the onerous legwork and research that the editor looks forward to about as much as a root canal.

CHAPTER 2: SWEETHEART, GET ME REWRITE

For example: you just happen to be in possession of a list of the most powerful aerospace engines on the market, ranked according to horsepower. (Lists! Rankings! And the editorial staff didn't have to compile it! Give that drooling editor a napkin!) Offer to make this list available, because you're such a helpful guy and, besides, you really admire the editor and the publication. And, as you're making this list available, manage to smoothly slip in your own need: a mention of your client, a quote from your client's CEO, whatever. Just don't be so gauche as to make the mutual back scratching overt and obvious. It's just a case of two buddies helping each other out.

When you're developing story ideas for reporters, don't just think in terms of "spot news" — something that just happened that demands to be covered. Think in terms of features the reporter could write about interesting people, trends in the field and "tick-tocks" (minute-by-minute accounts of something dramatic that happened in the not-so-distant past). Here are a few steps to follow:
» Recommend web sites, statistics and third-party analysts.
» Fax or email other articles related to the subject in question.
» Provide sources and their contact information — phone numbers and email addresses.

Act as an enabler for the media's laziness. Despite all of their tough talk about being the Fourth Estate and the guardians of society's liberties, many journalists crave the easy way out. They instinctively seek the path of least resistance. Take them by the hand and walk them down this path. They will love you for it, and reward you with ink for your message.

Use similar tactics for stories that are already published. When you see a story on a topic that falls within your self-interest, call or email the writer. Praise the writer, for his rare insights and uncommonly stylistic

THE CONFESSIONS OF AN INK-STAINED WRETCH

prose. Demonstrate that you actually read the article and understand the subject matter. Offer additional information that could serve as the basis for a follow-up story. Not only do reporters love help with stories, but they also love to milk existing stories for as many follow-up pieces as possible. The news hole is an insatiable beast, which means many reporters seek to recycle (the polite word is "re-purpose") existing research.

Don't underestimate the power of small, personal acts. There's too much reliance nowadays on email. Take the trouble to cut out an article that may be of interest to the editor you're trying to influence, and send it via snail mail — with a short, witty, handwritten personal note attached. Quick references to sports, hobbies or family are a great way to cement the bond. For example:

> Jerry -
>
> Howdy! I thought you'd find this story on HMO fraud interesting, as well as useful for your upcoming cover story on the health care industry. I underlined a particularly compelling paragraph on page 26. Hope this helps! I know a couple of sources in health care that could assist your reporting. Call or email me if you want their contact info.
>
>   – John
>   555-1212
>   jpersinos@newspaper.com
>   P.S. Go Sox!

The crucial element here is the follow up. If you don't receive a call or email in a timely fashion, then place an innocuous phone call. "Hey Jerry! Wazzup buddy! Did you get that article I sent you?" You must

CHAPTER 2: SWEETHEART, GET ME REWRITE

always walk that razor's edge, between persistence and boorishness. When does assertive follow up lapse into obnoxious pestering? It's hard to say; it's almost as difficult as determining the difference between dating and stalking. Let your conscience — or your restraining order — be your guide.

In an era when everyone leans on email as a crutch, a handwritten note conveys manners, consideration and thoughtfulness. It grabs attention and it establishes trust. And you know what? It makes your job more fun. Their atrocious table manners aside, journalists are human beings, and they're enjoyable companions. Don't treat them as marks; treat them as colleagues and peers. You just might make a friend for life.

Remember to be polite and friendly. I used to work in an office where casual dress was the norm, which is often the case with reporters when they're not out covering a story. A job applicant came in for an interview with me, glanced at my blue jeans, and said with a sneer: "Thanks for dressing up for me!" I kept the interview short and then tossed his resume into the trash — not because of personal pique, but because of the poor judgment that he showed. A socially inappropriate remark or behavior can cost you plenty. In this case, it cost the guy a job. His worst enemy was his own big mouth.

Incorporate follow ups as a systemic part of your daily routine. Carve out a certain amount of time every day, during which you hit the phones, instant messenger and email, to ping various journalists to whom you've already sent information. These journalists live in a swirling vortex of information and pressure and it's easy for them to forget you. Out of sight, out of mind. If you mail an article, and let too much time elapse before contact, your article will become forgotten fish wrap before you know it.

THE CONFESSIONS OF AN INK-STAINED WRETCH

10 TIPS FOR PLACING AN OP-ED PIECE

Not everyone has pockets as deep as an oil company's. If you don't want to pony up the cash to buy ad space on an op-ed page, you can accomplish the same feat by using these sure-fire tactics:

1. Set up a visit with the editorial board. Almost every publication has one; check the names and titles on the masthead. A common mistake is to simply throw an unsolicited editorial over the transom and ask that it get ink; you stand about as much success with this tactic as you do in getting an unsolicited screenplay made into a big-budget movie. *Fuhgeddaboudit.*

2. Search archives to see whether the publication already has staked out a view on the issue at hand. If so, then wait for a timely event, a "news peg," that's related to the issue, and then request a meeting with the board to make your pitch. Incorporate this event into your arguments. When dealing with the press, always consider timeliness. Too often, marketers promote ideas that are generic "evergreens" with no newsworthiness or sense of urgency.

3. Consider bringing a group of like-minded people with you to the meeting, a tactic that will convey the impression that there's a broader constituency or groundswell of opinion behind your position.

HOW TO PLACE AN OP-ED PIECE

Many people mistakenly think that "op-ed" stands for opinion-editorial. Actually, it refers to editorials, written by staff, syndicated writers and guest writers that run "opposite editorial" — i.e., opposite the publication's main, institutional editorial. *The New York Times* pio-

CHAPTER 2: SWEETHEART, GET ME REWRITE

4. When seeking an appointment with the editorial board, include a press release and a concise fact sheet of bulleted talking points.

5. Keep your message focused and easy to understand. Don't burden the board with elaborate PowerPoint presentations or long-winded white papers. Don't lapse into "wonkish" dialogue that's dry, academic and overly complex. Avoid inside baseball.

6. Distill your message into a few easily understood "drivers" (see page 42) and present these drivers in a punchy manner. To persuade any editorial board, your themes must be brought down to earth in a practical and easily grasped manner. Emphasize universal themes, such as fairness, prices, safety, jobs, etc.

7. Don't come off as a know-it-all. You don't have to be an expert, merely well informed.

8. Be measured; appear rational. Don't come off as a firebrand or an ideologue

9. Don't be arrogant. Listen to feedback; respond respectfully and diplomatically to disagreements.

10. After you leave, send a follow-up "thanks-for-your-time-look-forward-to-hearing-from-you" note to the editorial board. Keep pinging them, in a restrained way, until you get definitive word as to whether your piece will run.

neered the op-ed page concept. The man who pioneered the exploitation of the op-ed page was an innovator named Herb Schmertz.

THE CONFESSIONS OF AN INK-STAINED WRETCH

> The sensibilities of tabloid journalism dominate all journalism today. While circulation for news-related publications continues its decline, the circulation numbers for celebrity magazines continue to soar. Most news is reduced to easily grasped melodramatic stories, with heroes and bad guys.

The late, great Schmertz was the public relations genius at Mobil Corp. (now ExxonMobil) who blazed the trail for "planted" editorials. During the 1970s and 1980s, when oil companies were getting bad press for "obscene profits," Schmertz purchased advertising space in the quality press, notably the Holy of Holies — *The Times* op-ed page — to run editorials sponsored by Mobil.

Today, oil companies are again under political pressure (very mild pressure) for racking up record profits from high energy prices, and sure enough, ExxonMobil's op-ed "columns" regularly run in *The Times,* defending these profits.

The groundbreaking Mobil editorials of yore made no bones about being paid advertising, by prominently depicting at the top Mobil's blue and red logo (a minimalist masterpiece of mid-1960s pop design, by the way). Now a familiar tactic, the idea was new at the time — and it worked. Through sheer dint of cash, Mobil became a player on the op-ed page, alongside Scotty Reston and William Safire. Mobil successfully added its conservative, corporatist voice to the conversation.

CHAPTER 2: SWEETHEART, GET ME REWRITE

A more insidious form of "buying opinion" occurred during the second Bush administration when it purchased favorable news coverage of its education policies by making payments to conservative black commentator Armstrong Williams, and hired Ketchum Inc., a public relations company, to monitor and analyze media coverage of the GOP. Purchasing propaganda in this manner is not only beyond the wallets of most marketers — it's also illegal, according to the General Accounting Office, the independent non-partisan accountability arm of Congress. Since the Williams scandal broke, several other names of "bought" columnists have come to light.

Bribery is so crude! It breaks the law and, more importantly, undermines your credibility. There's a better way to get your message onto the op-ed page. As the earlier sidebar explains, you can mold public opinion and still be above-board, fair and legal about it.

HITTING YOUR TARGETS

Customize your message to the right media. As a journalist, one of my pet peeves is when a PR hack bombards me with a pitch that isn't appropriate for my publication or beat. It's a common practice that's so lazy, it borders on disrespect. Here's an effective (but by no means inclusive) list of the best sources for conducting your upfront targeting:
» Bacon's Media Directories (www.bacons.com/directories/maindirectories.asp)
» Broadcasting & Cable Yearbook (www.bowker.com)
» Burrelle's Media Directory (www.burrelles.com/indexmd.html)
» Media Finder (www.mediafinder.com)
» Gebbie Press All-in-One Directory (www.gebbieinc.com)
» NewsLink (www.newslink.org)
» MediaMapOnline (www.mediamaponline.com)

THE CONFESSIONS OF AN INK-STAINED WRETCH

> In an era when everyone leans on email as a crutch, a handwritten note conveys manners, consideration and thoughtfulness. It grabs attention and establishes trust. It also makes your job more fun. Their atrocious table manners aside, journalists are human beings and enjoyable companions.

If you worked hard to influence a story and it gets bumped, don't take it personally. Stories get moved around, dramatically edited and rescheduled all the time. The editorial process is a rough-and-tumble business, and it requires a thick skin. Take setbacks in stride; be stoic in the face of disappointment. If your message was riding on a particular story and the story gets spiked or delayed, don't whine about it. Dispassionately ask when you can expect to see the story eventually run. You want to help the editor, but you don't want to tell him his business and come off as a kibitzer. He has enough to worry about, without your bitching and moaning.

So how do you frame your story so that it jumps ahead of the hundreds of others that are contending for the editor's, producer's or blogger's attention? Read on.

Chapter 3

YOU BURIED THE LEDE – AGAIN!

How to Practice Journalism Better Than the Journalists Do

One of my favorite books is the witty and insightful *On Advertising*, written by Madison Avenue legend David Ogilvy. He determined that about six times as many people read news articles than read advertisements.

Nothing confers greater credibility on your message than having it picked up by the press. So how do you go about it? By applying Ogilvy's same general rule to the press itself. Don't manipulate the press; co-opt it.

> "THE QUESTION IS," SAID ALICE, "WHETHER YOU CAN MAKE WORDS MEAN SO MANY DIFFERENT THINGS."
> – Lewis Carroll, *Through the Looking Glass*

THE CONFESSIONS OF AN INK-STAINED WRETCH

> Most people (including the press) are too busy, distracted, impatient and lazy to focus on a long, complicated message. You must serve up your message the same way you serve up a microwave snack: make it fast, tasty and easy to swallow.

Journalists will pay greater attention to your message, and perhaps use it as a springboard for their own stories, if your message takes on all of the trappings of news. Find a timely "news peg" on which to hang your message, and then write your press releases and individualized pitches in standard newspaper/wire service style.

Determine the "focus" of what you want to say, summarize the focus in extremely tight and direct language, and put that focus within the first paragraph. Tighter is always better. (See upcoming "The 10 Rules to Writing a Killer Press Release," page 63.) Also, as a standard reference, buy a copy of the Associated Press Stylebook and religiously follow its strictures. My "Rules" on press releases are an example of the guidance you'd find in the AP Stylebook.

You can order an AP Stylebook through www.inkstained confessions.com. Even if it's only on an unconscious level, journalists will recognize that your writing "follows the rules," which means they'll be more likely to pay attention and give it credence.

To lend greater credibility to your release, quote third-party analysts who can buttress your point. Go to the trouble of contacting and

CHAPTER 3: YOU BURIED THE LEDE – AGAIN!

actually interviewing "subject matter experts" who are relevant to the topic at hand. These experts include trade magazine editors, academics, consultants and think tank staffers. Pinpoint analysts who work for high-profile organizations that are independent and unaffiliated. Journalists use this trick all the time; that's why you read and see the same, incestuous circle of quotemongers all the time. These self-promoting analysts know that, to get their names out into the public realm, they only need to return reporter's phone calls and demonstrate a knack for distilling complex issues into compelling sound bites. Use the same tactic yourself.

Need an "independent" analyst to support your focus and confer greater credibility to your marketing? Take him to an expensive restaurant. After the second glass of wine, he'll give you any quote you need.

THE 10 RULES TO WRITING A KILLER PRESS RELEASE
Here are the 10 time-honored rules to writing an effective press release:

1. PUNCH UP THE HEADLINE
■ Your headline must be as punchy and colorful as possible without exaggerating or stretching the truth. The headline must be tight as a drum, using as few words as possible, but it must also convey the topic of the article in a way that grips the reader's attention. A general rule of news story writing is to use active words and to avoid the passive; that's especially true in the headline. In the headline, emphasize those aspects that are the timeliest and most dramatic. Avoid conjunctions; get to the point in telegraphic style.

2. FOLLOW THE INVERTED PYRAMID
■ The "inverted pyramid" represents the old school of news reporting. As far as I'm concerned, it's timeless and always worth obeying. To understand the metaphor, envision an upside-down pyramid. The broad base is filled with the most important information, and the

THE CONFESSIONS OF AN INK-STAINED WRETCH

narrow tip is filled with the least important. Unfortunately, many journalists no longer follow this basic structure of writing. Too often, I have to wait until, say, the 12th paragraph before I get to the actual lede, because the writer wants to impress me with his novelistic technique and is setting the scene. When I want to read a short story, I'll pick up a volume of Dostoevsky or Fitzgerald. When I want to be informed, I pick up a newspaper or a press release.

3. WRITE A FOCUSED AND COMPELLING LEDE

The lead, or first paragraph of the story, is spelled in journalese as the "lede." There are many stories as to why, some of them urban legends and apocryphal, to be sure, but the most widely accepted anecdote is that, in the early days of wire services, blue pencil references to "the lead" were purposely misspelled by editors, so they wouldn't be confused with actual copy. The lede is the most important aspect of your press release or news story. If you don't attract the attention of readers in the lede, you never will.

The lede should start with a "dateline," which denotes the place where it was issued and the date. Use lean, unadorned, adjective-free language in the lede. (To see examples of notable ledes I have written over the years, go to my web site, www.inkstainedconfessions.com.) Eschew purple prose. Grab your readers by the lapels, right away. A lede can be anywhere from one to three sentences — four, at the most.

Less is more. You can convey enormous impact with just a few words. I turn to the Bible for a powerful case in point: "Jesus wept." Can you make that statement any better, by adding words?

A lede must never be boring. As I say above, make your lede a "grabber." Burned in my memory is a journalism professor at Boston University, the great Jonathan Klarfeld, who once commanded our class to write a news story from our notes. He ambled around the

CHAPTER 3: YOU BURIED THE LEDE – AGAIN!

room, peering over our shoulders, as we pecked away on our manual typewriters (yes, manual typewriters). He suddenly stopped by my desk and punched me, hard, on the shoulder. "That's a dead-ass lede, Persinos!" I tore the carbon-backed paper (yes, carbon-backed paper) out of the carriage and started again.

As I was writing this chapter, a press release turned up in my in-box with this headline: AMERICANS KNOW MORE ABOUT THE SIMPSONS THAN THEY DO ABOUT THE CONSTITUTION! This made me laugh, and I read the release to find out more. If the headline had been something bland like AMERICANS STILL UNAWARE OF THEIR CONSTITUTIONAL RIGHTS, I might have just deleted it.

Your lede is everything. Bad lede = bad press release. But before you can write the lede, you must determine the focus.

4. DETERMINE THE FOCUS, AND STICK TO IT

Most writers get into trouble with a story or press release because they start writing before they figure out what they want to say. Before you hit the keyboard, take a deep breath and think about the piece you're about to write. What's it really about? Do you have enough information? Summarize, in your head, the theme — the point. If you can't, then maybe you need to gather more information.

As mentioned in the Foreword to this book, there are three rules to effective press release/news story writing:
1. Focus
2. Focus
3. Focus

www.inkstainedconfessions.com

THE CONFESSIONS OF AN INK-STAINED WRETCH

The second paragraph fleshes out and reiterates the themes posited in the lede; it's called the "billboard-graph" (or "nut-graph") because it serves as a billboard to advertise the core themes, the nut, of your story.

A common error is to write the release/story with the information conveyed in chronological order, as if it were a history term paper. One of the most annoying traits I've ever come across as an editor is when the writer puts the most relevant and timeliest information at the bottom of the story, compelling me to circle this bottom-dwelling paragraph and connect the circle to a big arrow that swings back to the beginning of the story. In the margin, in large cap letters, I will angrily scrawl the classic admonition: "You buried the lede!" Unfortunately, because burying the lede tends to be an ingrained bad habit, I will often be forced to add: "— again!"

5. LOCALIZE AND/OR NATIONALIZE

Sometimes, your release will target local or regional media, so include information that's relevant to the community. That said, you should strive to put the release into a broader context by nationalizing it. For example: why will a particular energy trend affect all consumers at the gas pump?

6. AVOID JARGON

Avoid acronyms, insider euphemisms and technical terminology. If your subject or audience is technology-intensive, you have no choice. But always try to go light on the jargon. Unless you're writing about extremely well known entities (e.g., the FBI or NASA), spell out acronyms on first reference. You don't want to assume too much knowledge on the audience's part, but by the same token, you don't want to be too elemental and come off as naïve. It's a delicate balancing act.

CHAPTER 3: YOU BURIED THE LEDE – AGAIN!

7. BE CONCISE

■ Your press release shouldn't be any longer than two pages (roughly 1,000 words). Preferably, you can convey your entire message in only one page. Believe me: very few reporters will read beyond two pages.

8. INCLUDE QUOTES, SELECTIVELY

■ Incorporate relevant comments from a minimum of one person and a maximum of three. Try to quote a recognized expert in the field you're covering (see Chapter Two). Reserve quotes for information that's conveyed in a conversational or colorful manner. A common mistake is to use quotes as a dumping ground for information. If the quote can be paraphrased as straight narrative, then do so. Using quotes to convey dry data is a common manifestation of lazy writing. Quotes should spice up the story.

9. PROOFREAD

■ Speaking of laziness, it amazes me how often I've seen spelling or typographical errors in a press release. Sloppy mistakes undermine the credibility of your release. It makes the reporter question the accuracy of the entire document. When I see a misspelled word or typo, I immediately toss the release into the trash. A while back, I was reading an article proposal by a writer who claimed to be an expert on "exchange-traded funds," a new type of mutual fund. Trouble is, all through the piece he called them "EFTs" rather than their actual acronym, "ETFs." He didn't get the assignment. In fact, I made a note of his name, and vowed to never use him as a writer for any topic.

It's helpful to have a second set of eyes look at anything you write; ask a colleague to proof it for you, as well. Chances are, they'll catch something you missed. Don't just proof or edit the finished release on your computer screen; print it out. When editing, I find it useful to grapple with actual ink and paper. Call me old fashioned, but language seems

THE CONFESSIONS OF AN INK-STAINED WRETCH

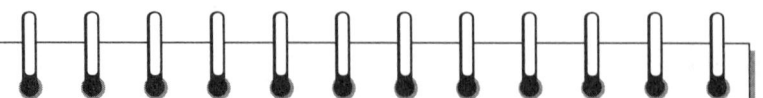

```
The "inverted pyramid" represents the
old school of news reporting. It's
timeless and always worth obeying.
Envision an upside-down pyramid; the
broad base is filled with the most
important information, and the narrow
tip is filled with the least impor-
tant. Unfortunately, many journalists
no longer follow this basic structure
of writing.
```

different on the printed page; my editorial "inner ear" picks up a different rhythm. When using a red pen on paper, I invariably find errors that had previously escaped my attention when I was scrolling on the computer screen.

10. LEAVE GUIDEPOSTS

» Include accessible contact information. Insert updated contact information in the upper right-hand corner. Reporters are under constant deadline pressure and, as such, they're impatient. Contacts must be easily accessible. Cell phone and email addresses are useful.

» Write "—more—" at the bottom of the page, if the release continues to an additional page. Write "page two" in the upper left-hand corner of the second page.

» Make it clear that your release is finished by inserting "—END—" at the bottom of the last page.

CHAPTER 3: YOU BURIED THE LEDE – AGAIN!

TIGHTER IS ALWAYS BETTER

In all of your correspondence with journalists, create prose that's concise and easily scanned. This is a good rule, regardless of whether your audience is a member of the media or a lay reader. Edit your copy several times; relentlessly prune deadwood. I used to have an editor who would cut my copy in front of me while murmuring to himself, "This can go ... This can go"... Now I do it to my own writing, and you should, too.

Strip every sentence to its simplest components. Avoid passive construction that makes the reader wonder who is doing what. Consistently strive for the active voice — it's more direct and compelling:

I will always cherish my memories of the newsroom.

This is far superior to:

My memories of the newsroom will always be cherished by me.

Also, the final words "by me" are extraneous. You can end the sentence on "cherished."

Convey statements strongly and declaratively. Don't be wimpy in your assertions. Instead of writing this:

She did not consider him to be very honest.

Write this:

She considered him dishonest.

www.inkstainedconfessions.com

THE CONFESSIONS OF AN INK-STAINED WRETCH

Remember: your reader has the attention span of a chihuahua on crystal meth. As I point out in Chapter One, the flickering images on the Boob Tube dominate our culture and all public discourse. Political advisers know this truth quite keenly and they apply it with unabashed zeal. Presidents are continually portrayed in "photo-ops" because images matter more than the spoken or written word. Boss Tweed, the leader of New York City's infamously corrupt Tammany Hall political machine in the mid-19th century, once said that newspaper criticism of his municipal administration didn't matter, because most of his political base was illiterate. What really hurt him, he said, were "those damn pictures" — i.e., the incisive and biting political cartoons of Thomas Nast, as exemplified by Nast's drawing of a robber baron with a sack of money for a head, with the caption: "The Brains."

Short attention spans, declining literacy, diminished intellectual discipline and low levels of education: that's the marketing ocean in which you must swim. As the general populace gets dumber, so do the journalists who allegedly "inform" it.

Consequently, don't make assumptions that the reader will "get it," just because you get it. Maybe you've connected the dots in your own head, but if you haven't connected the dots in your writing, then the reader will be confused. The reader isn't psychic. You need to explicitly make your point.

However, when using data from your notes, don't feel obligated to throw everything onto the page. A common mistake among reporters is to use every scrap of information. Don't be pushed around by your notebook. Judiciously use information that assists your theme, and get rid of the rest.

CHAPTER 3: YOU BURIED THE LEDE – AGAIN!

Laborious locutions weigh down your writing. Don't use them. Common examples include:
» at this point in time
» at the present time
» in order to
» currently
» presently
» the fact of the matter is
» in the final analysis
» I might add
» It should be pointed out

For example: The description of an event in a release assumes that it's current; you don't need to write "currently" or "presently." Just say what you have to say:

Energy legislation is pending. NOT: **Energy legislation is currently pending.**

Eliminate the conjunction "that" as often as possible. You'll be pleasantly surprised to discover how often you don't need the word.

Vigorously edit all of your copy. As you edit, you'll find that each new version is better than the previous one. As I've previously explained, carve out enough time in your schedule to secure a review of your writing by an objective third party, in the form of a friend or colleague. You can get too close to your writing; another person will provide objectivity and probably catch something you missed. Every writer, no matter how talented or experienced, needs an editor.

Don't fall in love with your ornate prose. For example, if writing a press release about tourism in Boston, you might be tempted to write something like this:

www.inkstainedconfessions.com

THE CONFESSIONS OF AN INK-STAINED WRETCH

For all the attention and accolades lavished on Boston's high-technology sector along Route 128, tourism remains an important segment of the city's economy. Beantown is jam-packed with internationally famous tourist attractions that draw enormous crowds of visitors every year. In 2006, the most popular destinations included Faneuil Hall and Quincy Market; the Old North Church; the "Cheers" pub; the North End; the Paul Revere House; the Boston Common and Public Garden; the Freedom Trail; and the Park Street Church. By visiting these storied places, out-of-town guests can truly experience the cosmopolitan and European flair of one of America's oldest and most revered cities.

The prose flows nicely, doesn't it? There's just one problem: no one will read it. Here's how the above paragraph should be written:

In 2006, some of the most-visited places in Boston included:
» Faneuil Hall and Quincy Market
» The Old North Church
» The "Cheers" pub
» The North End
» The Paul Revere House
» The Boston Common and Public Garden
» The Freedom Trail
» The Park Street Church

Get the picture? Less is more.

THE COMMON PITFALLS OF STYLE

No, I'm not referring to polyester slacks and mullets. In my experience as an editor, the following spelling and grammatical issues tend to surface the most often during the editing, proofing and design process. If

CHAPTER 3: YOU BURIED THE LEDE – AGAIN!

THE FIVE RULES FOR SOUND BITES

1. Make a list of all the concepts you want to convey; come up with a snappy word or two that encapsulates each concept. Make a list of those words, and then play with permutations of them — roughly akin to playing those refrigerator magnet word games.

2. Tailor your sound bite to your specific audience and situation. Don't make it too broad or generic.

3. Read aloud your sound bite; if it takes longer than 15 seconds, it's too long. Correspondingly, you should be able to fit a single sound bite on the back of your business card.

4. Try to use alliteration, the repetition of usually initial consonant sounds in two or more adjoining words or syllables. The famous phrase written by William Safire, for Spiro Agnew, is a classic of political alliteration: "nattering nabobs of negativism." Other classics include the supposed platforms of presidential candidates Al Smith ("Rum, Romanism and Rebellion") and George McGovern ("Amnesty, Acid and Abortion"). At least, that's what their opponents said.

5. Use rhymes combined with rhythm, e.g., Johnny Cochran's famous exhortation to the O.J. Simpson jury: "If the glove don't fit, you must acquit."

you violate these rules, it will hurt your credibility with the editor you're trying to influence.
» Email is spelled without a hyphen, lower case
» Web is upper-case; web site is two words, lower case
» No comma before "and" in a list

www.inkstainedconfessions.com

THE CONFESSIONS OF AN INK-STAINED WRETCH

```
Before you hit the keyboard, take a
deep breath and think about the piece
you're about to write. What's it
really about? Do you have enough
information? Summarize, in your head,
the theme - the point. If you can't,
then maybe you need to gather more
information.
```

» Be consistent in use of singular apostrophe ('s) versus plural (s')
» Spell out whole numbers below 10; use figures for 10 and above (this is a general rule — consult the AP stylebook for exceptions)
» Periods and other punctuation belong inside closed quotation marks
» Spell out first use of acronym, followed by acronym in parentheses, e.g.: Security Management Assessment (SMA). Exception: when the acronym is a household word, e.g.: FBI.
» E.g. means "for example" *(exempli gratia)* and should be spelled with periods, whereas i.e. means "that is" *(id est)* and should also be spelled with periods
» Antivirus is always "antivirus"
» No two-line subheads; they must fit on one line
» Titles: in general, confine capitalization to formal titles used directly before an individual's name; lower case and spell out titles when they are not used with an individual's name; capitalize formal titles when they are used immediately before one or more names
» When a compound modifier — two or more words that express a single concept — precedes a noun, use hyphens to link all the words in the compound except the adverb, very, and all adverbs that end in

CHAPTER 3: YOU BURIED THE LEDE – AGAIN!

"ly." Examples: *a first-quarter touchdown, a bluish-green dress, a very good time, an easily remembered rule*
» After: *no hyphen after this prefix when it is used to form a noun*
» When a phrase lists only a month and a year, do not separate the year with commas, e.g.: March 2005. Lower case all seasons (fall, winter, spring, summer)
» Omitted figures (such as 19 or 20, for centuries) should be expressed this way: The Class of '62

USING SOUND BITES

When interacting with the press, make sure all of your written collateral (press releases, emails, letters) and all of your verbal conversations incorporate plenty of sound bites. Admittedly, "sound bite" here is a misnomer, because in this context I'm also referring to the written word. But my point remains: you must develop an ingrained instinct whereby you distill complex issues into short, colorful phrases. Don't be afraid to play with words. Relish the flexibility of language. In speaking with reporters, revive the lost art of conversation — without wasting their time and becoming a windbag.

When Pat Buchanan argues with, say, Michael Kinsley on those insufferable TV gabfests, Buchanan always seems to get the best of Kinsley, even when Kinsley has a better argument. That's because Kinsley — ever the empathetic and philosophical liberal — delves into nuances and various shades of gray. Consequently, he comes off as a wishy-washy milquetoast. Meanwhile, the Jesuit-schooled Buchanan possesses black-and-white certitude and he sees the world in simple Manichean terms. He has no doubts; he expresses his views crisply, cleanly, concisely, confidently — and with plenty of snappy sound bites. Kinsley, with his lawyerly and analytical mind, often ends up on the losing end of the argument — even when he's right.

THE CONFESSIONS OF AN INK-STAINED WRETCH

The lesson? Regardless of your views, you must emulate Pat Buchanan's mode of delivery. Keep it simple, keep it punchy and demonstrate the courage of your convictions.

Most people (including the press) are too busy, distracted, impatient and lazy to focus on a long, complicated message. You must serve up your message the same way you serve up a microwave snack: make it fast, tasty and easy to swallow. Follow my five "sound bite rules," in the sidebar on page 73.

At some point, you'll probably have to move on from phone calls and emails to hosting an event for the press. The next chapter explains how — but be warned, our table manners aren't the greatest.

Chapter 4

ALL ABOARD THE GRAVY TRAIN

The Care and Feeding of Demanding Egotists

I miss Richard Nixon. His sweaty, sneering, shifty-eyed performances during press conferences were always the stuff of comic opera. Who can watch those old film clips without thinking of Dan Aykroyd's dead-on (and politically incorrect) impression?

> **"THE PRESS IS THE ENEMY."**
> – Richard Nixon

Aykroyd's Nixon: "Henry! We must pray! Whatsamatter, don't you pray, *Jew-boy?*"

Belushi's Kissinger: "Uh...Mr. President...Mr. President. Why don't we just put on our jammies and go sleepy-time, huh?"

Nixon's best-known press conference, immediately following his humiliating 1962 loss of the California gubernatorial contest to Pat Brown, is

THE CONFESSIONS OF AN INK-STAINED WRETCH

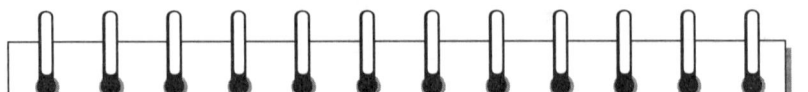

> Situate the press conference in close proximity to the media you invite. Avoid out-of-the-way locations that require driving directions or — heaven forbid! — mass transit. Most journalists express a fondness for mass transit in their writings, but only in terms of abstract public policy. Pick a venue that's widely known and easily accessible.

a classic example of how not to deal with the media. "You won't have Dick Nixon to kick around anymore," he said, his voice dripping with hatred, self-pity and bitterness. Ol' Tricky Dick could have used some couch work, that's for sure.

Of course, later presidents simply avoided dealing with the hated press by holding fewer and fewer conferences. If you circumvent and disrespect the press on a consistent basis, you stand a good chance of getting away with it — at first. But the bad karma will catch up with you. The press holds grudges and, in the end, it makes you pay. That's in large part why, 12 years after his infamous California press conference, Nixon gave...his presidential resignation speech.

Remember this, and remember it well: politicians and businesspeople come and go, but the Fourth Estate abides forever. The press, as feeble as it can sometimes be, always gets the last laugh.

CHAPTER 4: ALL ABOARD THE GRAVY TRAIN

It's fascinating to compare Nixon's tortuous performances during press conferences with those of John Kennedy. No matter how tough the questioning, Kennedy always exuded insouciant charm, literary wit and Ivy League aplomb. But you don't have to be Jack Kennedy to pull off a successful press conference.

Here are my basic rules for conducting any event for the press:

THE 20 RULES FOR A SUCCESSFUL PRESS EVENT

1. Serve food. My experience has shown that serving food at a press event exponentially boosts turnout. Reporters love freebies, especially those that can be consumed. Journalists like to brag that, if they play their cards right, they rarely have to buy their own meals. Scoring a free meal provides a perverse form of pride in my profession. A hot meal is preferable. Make sure there's lots of coffee. Most reporters are hopeless coffee addicts who crave caffeine's stimulation of the cerebral cortex.

2. Schedule the event in the late morning or afternoon. Not only do reporters like free food, they're also lazy. If you hold a press conference early in the morning, many of them won't show. Avoid rush hour.

3. Emphasize convenience. Situate the press conference in close proximity to the media you invite. Avoid out-of-the-way locations that require driving directions or — heaven forbid! — mass transit. Most journalists express a fondness for mass transit in their writings, but only in terms of abstract public policy. Choose a location that's widely known and easily accessible.

THE CONFESSIONS OF AN INK-STAINED WRETCH

> It's fascinating to compare Nixon's tortuous performances during press conferences with those of Kennedy. No matter how tough the questioning, Kennedy always exuded insouciant charm, literary wit and Ivy League aplomb. But you don't have to be Jack Kennedy to pull off a successful press conference.

4. **Pick a suitably impressive setting.** Your venue must communicate sufficient gravitas. Book a meeting room in a federal or state building, a press club, hotel, town hall or a courthouse.

5. **Issue a one-page press release announcing the event.** Don't send the release too late or too early. A common mistake is to send the release so far in advance, the press forgets about the event when it finally rolls around on the calendar. Time your press release to arrive on reporters' desks roughly a week before the event. Don't use the shotgun approach. Determine the appropriate media; target the right reporters, editors, news directors, managing editors, bureau chiefs, producers and assignment editors. Concisely state the reason of the conference, the person(s) presiding, issues to be covered, the newsworthiness of the event's theme and the credentials of those speaking. Remember the "Seven Message Drivers" in Chapter Two, page 42. In your release, underscore any colorful elements in your message — and convey those elements in the lede. Plan on serving food and coffee and mention these amenities within the release, toward the bottom.

CHAPTER 4: ALL ABOARD THE GRAVY TRAIN

6. **Follow up with personal contact.** There's a fine line between persistence and being a pest, but err on the side of being a pest. Attention spans, and memories, are short. After you send the press release, wait a decent interval — say, 48 hours — and follow-up with a phone call to each and every news outlet, to make sure that the appropriate person obtained and actually read your release. Make a personal pitch as to why your event is worth attending and why it's in the news outlet's self-interest to send a representative. Call one more time — the day before the event.

7. **Be an attentive host.** At the event itself, wear a cleanly pressed business suit and post yourself adjacent the door, with a big smile. Place an outsized guest book on a nearby table. Welcome attendees as they arrive and politely ask them to sign in. The guest book will later help you in your follow-up calls; it also will help you build a media list.

8. **Distribute background material.** The press absolutely loves it when you give them white papers, backgrounders and texts of the speakers' remarks. Hand them out at the door, or leave them in neat piles on a table — where reporters can't miss them, right next to the coffee urns. Background material means they don't have to take careful notes and they can daydream a bit. Your press conference isn't just a forum for them to receive information; it's also a nice little respite from the office. It's a chance to get away from their claustrophobic cubicles and from their overbearing bosses. It's even more effective if you distribute this material on a computer disk, because then all the reporter has to do is cut-and-paste. If the reporter is able to relax with his coffee and croissant, and not worry too much about taking notes, he or she will surely attend your next press conference.

9. **Start on time.** Reporters hate it when press conferences start late; they take it as a sign of sloppiness and disrespect. They took the trouble to schlep across town to your event, so they expect punctuality

THE CONFESSIONS OF AN INK-STAINED WRETCH

on your part. Launch the proceedings no more than five minutes after the pre-arranged start time.

10. **Demonstrate courtesy.** To kick off the event, stand at the podium and commend everyone for attending. The media's self-love knows no bounds. Thank them for gracing you with their divine presence. Acknowledge the busy nature of their important lives; show them that you're cognizant of their awful deadline pressure. But most importantly, remind them that there's lots of fresh coffee and muffins in the back (low fat muffins especially appeal to female reporters).

11. **Establish ground rules.** Make it clear ahead of time how and when questions should be asked. The press moves in packs, but it can also act like a mob. Don't allow reporters to hijack your press event. I've witnessed press conferences that veer out of control and it's an ugly sight. Say something to this effect: "We look forward to your questions and we want to ensure a lively give-and-take. However, to ask a question, first raise your hand. When called upon, only ask one question at a time, and I kindly ask the others to not interrupt anyone while they're speaking. We'll try to get to everyone's questions today, as time allows."

12. **Make a brief opening statement.** Relinquish the podium to the spokesperson and make sure he, or she, makes a brief opening statement of no longer than 10 minutes.

13. **Stimulate questions from the audience.** Ensure a robust give-and-take between the speaker and the audience. Prepare a list of questions for you to ask. If the conversation starts to lag, step in with your own questions to get the ball rolling again. Don't allow long-winded sermons, from either the press or the speaker. Beware of manifestos disguised as questions. If a member of the press mounts a soap-

CHAPTER 4: ALL ABOARD THE GRAVY TRAIN

box and starts pontificating, step in and say politely but firmly: "What's your question?" (When you do, be prepared for knowing and appreciative chuckles from the audience. But don't embarrass the questioner by playing to the crowd. It will backfire and make you look like a bully.)

14. **Refrain from arguing with questioners.** Don't allow yourself or anyone on your team, to get dragged into an argument or debate with a press questioner. The effect will be disastrous. Regardless of whether you're right or wrong, if you demonstrate anger or impatience and begin verbally jousting with a reporter, you'll come off as an arrogant hot head and an enemy of the First Amendment. The crowd will turn on you like a pack of jackals. Keep your eye on the ball: the goal of your press event is to sell your message to the media, not to score debating points. At all times, convey the sense that the proceedings are under control and you are a cool, calm professional.

15. **Act like a team of professionals.** You may not know it, but the press is silently judging you and your cohorts who are running the press conference. Reporters are a judgmental bunch. If they think you're unprofessional or a lightweight, they're quick to wag a reproachful finger — behind your back, of course. If reporters determine that your press conference was poorly run, they'll let all of their cronies in the media know about it, diminishing your chances of getting a healthy turnout for your next event. If a reporter acts like a jerk, be polite. Never lose your cool.

16. **Get your facts straight and convey them dispassionately.** I'll never forget a press conference I attended when I was covering environmental issues. A liberal advocacy group was accusing Alcoa of violating environmental laws. Suddenly, the CEO of Alcoa walked in unannounced and started disputing the assertions! He argued that

www.inkstainedconfessions.com

THE CONFESSIONS OF AN INK-STAINED WRETCH

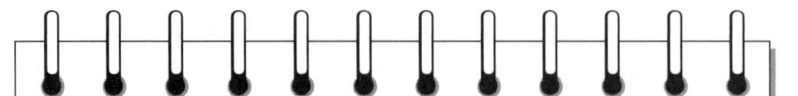

> The media's self-love knows no bounds. Thank them for gracing you with their divine presence. Acknowledge the busy nature of their important lives; show them that you're cognizant of their awful deadline pressure. But most importantly, remind them that there's fresh coffee and muffins in the back.

Alcoa had violated the law, but not as severely as the group was claiming. The CEO's argument actually had some merit, but his point was lost amid the drama. A few hours later, the group's press officer called reporters to "clarify" the situation, and then probably went back to cleaning out his desk. Of course, the assembled journalists, always eager to focus on conflict, wrote about the CEO's disruptive appearance, not the nuanced substance of the group's charges. Alcoa's CEO took a bad situation and made it far worse, by shooting from the hip.

17. **Keep your message focused.** Strive for one overriding message, delivered by one messenger. Before your speaker begins, "credentialize" him or her in your opening remarks by briefly citing their CV.

18. **Decisively end the proceedings.** Don't let the press conference just peter out with a whimper. Pay close attention to the dynamic and energy of the room. If it looks like the press is starting to run out of questions and it is losing interest, say loudly: "Okay, it looks like we're running out of time. Last question?" And then, after the last

CHAPTER 4: ALL ABOARD THE GRAVY TRAIN

question, thank everyone again for coming and say you're available if they require additional information.

19. **Set aside time for the television cameras.** I've always been amused by the way television camera crews dominate a room the instant they saunter in. Everyone snaps to attention when they see a camera crew. You must bow to this unavoidable reality. Buttonhole the TV crew immediately before the event; make sure all of their needs are met. Determine the camera crew's leader (it's usually the most self-important and slovenly person in the group). Assure him or her that the speaker will be available after the event to submit to a TV interview. Pick a convenient corner in the room for TV interviews and apprise both the camera crew and the speaker that they should convene in that corner, after the press conference has formally concluded.

20. **Send a thank-you note afterwards.** To each reporter who attended, immediately email (or snail mail) a personal message of appreciation for attending your event. During the event, take careful record of who asked questions. To those who did, praise their aggressiveness and emphasize the uncommon acuity of their questions. Flatter their probing intellect. Imply that the Republic rests easier because of their eternal vigilance. Make your services available; tell them that you can send them any further data they require for their stories.

SAMPLE RELEASE FOR PRESS EVENT

Below is an example of a release that I wrote to promote a live event that my company, Larstan Business Reports, conducted in Chicago. One reason I've singled out this release is to demonstrate the flexibility of language: with the right words, you can justify anything.

www.inkstainedconfessions.com

THE CONFESSIONS OF AN INK-STAINED WRETCH

This event, which went on to become a huge success, was rescheduled from October to December. The event was initially in trouble and lacked sponsors. We needed to buy time to perform more selling, but changing dates is a tricky business. Rather than sound defensive, I chose wording that made the rescheduling seem like a virtue that Larstan pursued for the greater good of everyone involved. I'll let my prose speak for itself. The result was that we got press coverage that helped generate a critical mass of sponsors.

Note well: the "call to action" is placed within the second paragraph and reiterated again in the last paragraph. Remember: "you gotta grab 'em early, and then tell 'em what ya already told 'em." Reiteration is the key to successful communication.

LARSTAN
BUSINESS REPORTS

INDUSTRY SUMMIT TO ADDRESS RFID CHALLENGES WITH GROUNDBREAKING RESEARCH

Washington, DC, Oct. 4 —

Top business executives are gathering to address urgent questions raised by the rapid spread of Radio Frequency Identification (RFID) — questions that can only be answered by newly gathered, proprietary research.

"RFID: Focus on the Future," an executive roundtable, has changed its date from October and will now be held Dec. 11-12 at the Chicago Omni Hotel, to accommodate an extensive RFID research effort launched this week by Larstan Business Reports. For more about the event: http://www.larstan.net/RFIDroundtable1.htm.

CHAPTER 4: ALL ABOARD THE GRAVY TRAIN

This research will entail in-depth questioning of medium-to-large sized manufacturers, distributors and consumer retailers concerning RFID implementation, in the consumer packaged goods (CPG), retail, pharmaceutical, automotive and transportation sectors in North America. The results of this research will shed light on RFID from all perspectives that are relevant to RFID users and vendors, including the business objectives, technical requirements and financial benefits of RFID.

"Assembling the industry's 'best and brightest' in one room is expected to result in a practical discussion that provides business case studies, implementation strategies and deployment lessons," says panelist Mike Crane, senior director, technology practice, Cisco Systems, Inc.

Panelist Walt DuLaney, CEO of Adaptive RFID, Inc., says the combination of roundtable discussion with proprietary research will substantially increase the RFID industry's knowledge. "This exclusive roundtable will be a closed-door collaboration of the leading minds in RFID, to help managers sort through the uncertainty that surrounds RFID." DuLaney says. "We will find tangible answers to pressing issues."

The survey results will be presented and discussed at the roundtable event in December. Produced by Larstan, this roundtable is a "must attend" event for RFID users and solution providers. Insiders will engage in a candid dialogue about the perils and promise of this spreading technology, as it affects key vertical markets. Program components also will include a keynote address, networking receptions and media Q&A sessions.

Following the roundtable, Larstan will publish a complete report — a technical, financial, operational and market impact analysis — that's based on the insights and survey results conveyed during the discussion.

THE CONFESSIONS OF AN INK-STAINED WRETCH

On the Agenda: Urgent RFID Topics
Topics on the roundtable agenda will include:
- The competitive advantages of being an early adopter of RFID.

- The profitable possibilities now available for RFID vendors.

- The applications that insiders predict will most help consumers embrace the use of RFID technology in everyday life.

- How RFID end users can choose the appropriate middleware, application software and management tools.

- How point-of-sale (POS) printer and scanner makers can foster greater operational efficiency and functionality at the POS level, to deliver "one-stop" solutions for retailers.

- The status of mandates and how to meet them.

- The ins-and-outs of business process modification for successful ROI in RFID.

- The advantages of RFID implementation for unit applications, as opposed to the entire supply chain.

Contact: John Persinos 240-396-0007 ext. 904; jpersinos@larstan.net. For more about the event: http://www.larstan.net/RFIDroundtable1.htm

CHAPTER 4: ALL ABOARD THE GRAVY TRAIN

AN AMERICAN (EXPRESS) IN PARIS

In this impersonal age of online communcations and the virtual extended enterprise, the in-person press event carries an extra wallop. Journalists love trade shows, press conferences and other live venues — if they're done right and with the proper amenities, as I've explained in this chapter. If the event is compelling enough for a journalist to bring his or her spouse, all the better. Don't underestimate the impetus and motivation often provided by a journalist's better half.

I'll never forget my wife's response when I resigned as editor-in-chief of *Rotor & Wing* magazine, to take another job. When she heard that I was leaving the world's premier rotorcraft publication — which necessitated the relinquishing of my expense account — she pursed her lips and scrunched up her nose. "Gee, does that mean we won't be attending the Paris Air Show anymore?" Yes, dear, I responded. Aviation companies would be deprived of my presence at press conferences — and the clothing stores of Paris would be deprived of my American Express.

In my next chapter, I'll look at the "punditocracy." These thumb-sucking columnists are perhaps the laziest and most biased journalists of all — which can make them easy prey for a skilled marketing attack. And you don't even have to serve them food.

Chapter 5

THE RISE OF THE PUNDITOCRACY

All About Those Self-Important Talking Head Blowhards

It all started with John McLaughlin, the former Catholic priest turned founding father of the political television slugfest. The success of "The McLaughlin Report" spawned a host of imitators and forever transformed the nature of public discourse. An

> **"LIFE'S BUT A WALKING SHADOW, A POOR PLAYER THAT STRUTS AND FRETS HIS HOUR UPON THE STAGE AND THEN IS HEARD NO MORE."**
> – Macbeth

unflagging conservative, McLaughlin as a priest was a fierce defender of

THE CONFESSIONS OF AN INK-STAINED WRETCH

> Truth is no obstacle to opinion. It's staggering the amount of outright lies, disinformation, agitprop, and spin that's prevalent on news talk shows. If you have a self-interested message to trumpet, don't be shy. Television has killed reality. More to the point, the line between "fact" and "opinion" has been blurred.

Richard Nixon during the nadir of Watergate — hence his nickname at the time, "Fighting Father McLaughlin."

I'm old enough to remember a gentler version of "The McLaughlin Report," called "Agronsky & Company." Hosted during the 1970s on public television by veteran broadcast newsman Martin Agronsky, the show was a veritable Greek symposium compared to the food fights on TV today. Regardless, the screaming matches on TV these days are undoubtedly bad for democracy. They cast more heat than light and emphasize emotional issues — typically, cultural wedge issues — over substantive policy analysis.

The essence of drama is conflict, which means these shows must create strife to remain entertaining. In today's society, the biggest sin is to bore people. Michael Kinsley is the brilliant neoliberal commentator who once served as editor of the online magazine *Slate*, as well as editor of the print magazines *Harper's* and *The New Republic*. Kinsley revealed that, during his stint as the "left" voice on CNN's

CHAPTER 5: THE RISE OF THE PUNDITOCRACY

"Crossfire," the producer of the show would sometimes yell into his earpiece: "Get mad!"

The instant, fatuous punditry of the bow-tied weenies you see on television has debased journalism, yet I can't deny that these shows are influential. In selling your message, you can't afford to ignore them. For you, they are a necessary evil. Television defines reality; if something didn't appear on television, it never happened. This book is designed to help you create a strategy that makes you a part of the conversation.

As a newsman who paid his dues practicing old-school print journalism, I particularly resent the pretty boys and bottle blondes who show up as pundits, without any previous publishing experience. Some of them get a titular position (no pun intended) on a publication to provide a phony credential, to justify their appearance on television. Many of these bloviating morons couldn't write their way out of a paper bag, and yet they wield influence on millions of people because they flap their gums in front of a camera.

But as they say on Wall Street: you can't buck the trend. These are the rules of media life in the first part of the 21st century. If you want to be an effective marketer and PR professional, you must play by these rules. Besides, who doesn't like to see themselves on television? It's the ultimate confirmation of success and it sure impresses your mom.

Television also gives your other press efforts longer life — it gives them legs. Once your message has appeared on television, the mere fact of its appearance becomes news in itself. Simply reiterating your message on a television talk show is worthy of a brand new press release that trumpets your appearance and drops names like crazy. It gives your message enormous credibility.

THE CONFESSIONS OF AN INK-STAINED WRETCH

The assumption is that if you managed to get past the gatekeepers at a television studio, you must have something on the ball. After enough appearances, the illusion starts to feed on itself. As I previously pointed out, there was a time when people became celebrities because they accomplished something noteworthy. Nowadays, a person becomes a celebrity simply for being famous. Get your foot in the door once or twice, and you've got it made. The trick is getting noticed the first time and then maintaining your momentum.

13 STEPS FOR GETTING YOUR MUG ON TELEVISION

So, how do you get your mug on the tube? Here are my 13 steps to becoming a TV pundit:

1. **Determine how the talk show prefers to receive a pitch.** As always, don't cold call your point person without learning the lay of the land. Does the show you've picked prefer emails, a downloadable application form, a fax or a phone call? Don't pursue a shotgun approach; tailor your pitch to the audience.

2. **Determine the point person.** Don't contact the first muckety-muck you find on a masthead. Figure out who specifically receives pitches. It might not be the producer; it may be the producer's assistant or some glorified clerk with an impressive-sounding title, like "managing editor" or "associate producer." If you send your pitch to the wrong person, it will probably grow cobwebs in an overstuffed inbox.

3. **Practice before contact.** Talk show producers are brutally overworked and notoriously impatient. You have a nanosecond to make a favorable impression. Before you contact him or her, practice your pitch on a colleague. Before you stick your head in the lion's maw, get a reality check and revise your pitch accordingly.

CHAPTER 5: THE RISE OF THE PUNDITOCRACY

4. **Initiate contact by faxing, emailing or express mailing your pitch and backgrounder.** Get hard copy material, especially your professional photo, in their hands from the start. A bio with a photo (either a hard copy photo sent by overnight mail, or a high-resolution JPG sent by email) will get their attention, especially if you're reasonably attractive person. The hard copy collateral provides your springboard for future and more intimate contact.

5. **Knock their socks off.** What's your pitch? Make it immediate and compelling. The focus of a conventional press release must be timely and different, but your pitch to a television producer has got to really grab 'em. Your story must be unique and you must be the only expert in the world who can do it justice. The topic must easily lend itself to visuals. It should be a simple linear narrative that's TV-friendly — a story with a beginning, middle and end.

6. **Provide talking points with your topic.** Within your pitch, in addition to spelling out your topic, draw up a list of potential questions and answers. It shows you've thought through your performance and you're prepared. Don't ostentatiously flog a company, product, service or book. If you do, you'll come off as a media hound and huckster. Stick to the substance of the topic.

7. **Provide a one-page bio.** More than ever, it's important to humanize your CV. You are selling more than your ideas; you're selling yourself. Provide a one-page backgrounder, as if you were an actor auditioning for a part. Attach a professionally taken headshot and emphasize your previous speaking gigs. Convey the sense that you have an attractive persona. Minimize in the talk show producer's mind any notion that you are an unknown quantity or a risk. Don't make your bio too long and be sure to leave out a lot of irrelevant information. Keep your CV short, sweet and succinct.

www.inkstainedconfessions.com

THE CONFESSIONS OF AN INK-STAINED WRETCH

> The instant, fatuous punditry of the bow-tied weenies you see on television has debased journalism, yet these shows are influential. In selling your message, you can't afford to ignore them. For you, they are a necessary evil. Television defines reality; if something didn't appear on television, it never happened.

8. **Examine the gamut of potential venues.** Do some research and pinpoint the show that's most appropriate for your message. Some specialize in pure horserace politics; others focus on law, crime or media. Target the show that's best suited for you. Do a little digging and determine the sort of topics these shows tend to favor. Talk show web sites are good places to start your homework.

9. **Follow up with a phone call.** Maybe you're calling on your own behalf, or on behalf of a client. Regardless, a day or two after sending your material, you should call the producer to sell yourself (or your client) and your idea. This phone call is crucial because it's your big chance to show how articulate and engaging you are. Don't ham it up too much, but it's incumbent on you to be lively, witty and well spoken. Think of yourself as an actor who is auditioning for a part.

10. **Call attention to any speaking experience.** If you're a neophyte to television, the producer will be wary of booking you. You can counteract this reticence by emphasizing any presentations

CHAPTER 5: THE RISE OF THE PUNDITOCRACY

you've made. You want to convey the impression that you're not shy, you won't suffer performance anxiety and you're quick on your feet. If you're a relative unknown to the airwaves, the producer is rolling the dice on you. Diminish the sense of risk by providing references that attest to your intelligence and powers of articulation.

11. **Watch the show before making your pitch.** Not only is this a good idea from a substantive standpoint, but it also gives you ammunition to stroke the producer's vanity. Make a point of referring to a previous show and talk knowledgeably about how great it was. Sounds obvious, but believe me: everyone, especially TV producers, likes to get their egos boosted. By all press accounts, John McLaughlin makes kissing his ass a major prerequisite for appearing on his show.

12. **Send a thank you note after your appearance.** Courtesy counts. As I write in my acknowledgements, one of the worst human qualities is ingratitude. The producer did you a big favor by granting you precious entry to television. By showing your appreciation, you'll increase your odds of getting invited back. Add the producer's name to your Rolodex and make him or her a regular recipient of your schmooze efforts. Not only will this relationship help your own publicity efforts, it also will earn you greater "street cred" with fellow marketers. Dropping a TV producer's name goes a long way to making you seem powerful.

13. **Add the appearance to your resume.** If you're fortunate enough to get on television and survive the experience, immediately add it to your backgrounder. You've now got a notch on your belt. The experience will help you secure another TV appearance and the goal will get progressively easier. You will become a pundit — and a special circle of Hell, reserved just for TV pundits, will be waiting for you when you die.

www.inkstainedconfessions.com

THE CONFESSIONS OF AN INK-STAINED WRETCH

TV GABFEST DIRECTORY

Here's a comprehensive (but by no means exhaustive) listing of the most influential news and political shows on TV broadcast and cable. These shows are the loudest megaphones for the braying "punditocracy."

You can get more information, and a web address, for each of these shows at http://www.polisource.com/links/audio_video.shtml. This handy web site also lists the multitude of talk/news radio programs around the country, with hotlinks.

Inside Politics
Wolf Blitzer Reports
Lou Dobbs Tonight
American Morning
Anderson Cooper 360°
Paula Zahn Now
CNN Saturday Morning
CNN Sunday Morning
CNN Daybreak
Larry King Live
Late Edition
People in the News
Reliable Sources
Inside Washington
The Chris Matthews Show
Hardball with Chris Matthews
Face the Nation
The McLaughlin Group
John McLaughlin's One on One
Meet the Press

CHAPTER 5: THE RISE OF THE PUNDITOCRACY

ABC's This Week
Washington Week
Bill O'Reilly
Fox Sunday
Your World with Neil Cavuto

TRICKS OF THE TRADE

In addition to my list of 13 how-to steps, there are other general tricks to remember when trying to grab the attention of TV and radio production staff responsible for booking guests.

Not every topic, whether it's a policy issue or book or whatever, is suitable for TV and radio promotion. Avoid the narrowly focused, and strive to emphasize generally popular categories: sex, relationships, personal finance, self-help, etc. Look for emerging trends and aim for the emotions. Make 'em laugh or cry — or make 'em afraid. Business-to-business appeal is the perspective that stands the greatest chance of success. Pick a timely B-to-B topic and bring it down to dollars and cents. Pitch the appropriate business show.

Newsworthiness is always a prerequisite, but a clever trick is to hitch your topic to a specific holiday. Try to pick a holiday that's less obvious, such as Labor Day, and instead highlight, say, National Secretaries' Day. Use a hook that a producer hasn't heard before.

It also works if you make yourself available as a last-minute stand-in. Back in the mid-1990s, when I was managing editor of *Campaigns & Elections* magazine, a producer with a cable TV talk show titled "America Talks" called me out of the blue and asked if my boss, the publisher of the magazine, was available to appear that night to discuss campaign finance reform. A controversial reform bill was wending its way through Congress and the talk show was looking for a political

THE CONFESSIONS OF AN INK-STAINED WRETCH

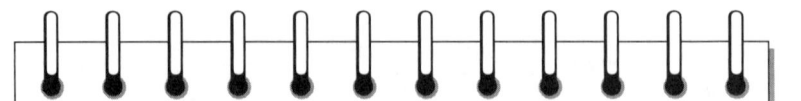

> ```
> Look for emerging trends and aim for
> the emotions. Make 'em laugh or cry -
> or make 'em afraid. Business-to-busi-
> ness appeal is the perspective that
> stands the greatest chance of success.
> Pick a timely B-to-B topic; bring it
> down to dollars and cents. Pitch the
> appropriate business show.
> ```

pundit to discuss its provisions, its chances and the topic in general. I informed the producer that, alas, my boss was unavailable and inaccessible because he was in transit on a business trip. I explained, however, that she was in luck because the perfect substitute was available — yours truly.

I leapt at the chance and immediately made my services available. During the phone call, I took pains to come off as a witty, amusing and deeply knowledgeable expert on all aspects of campaign finance. I exerted considerable energy in being engaging; I even added a little bass to my voice, a la Ted Baxter. I also played up my credentials as the managing editor of a political magazine headquartered on K Street itself.

The producer ate it all up and immediately sent a limo to our editorial offices, to whisk me to their TV studio for a live showing that evening. My appearance went fine. I suit up well and cameras don't intimidate me. I'm a natural born ham. But my practical point is this: if you want to get on TV, you must toot your own horn and lead with your personality. Try to show some charm, for chrissakes.

CHAPTER 5: THE RISE OF THE PUNDITOCRACY

YOU, TOO, CAN BECOME A BLUSTERING BLOVIATOR

As you gussy-up your marketing message for unveiling on television, always remember that these talk shows hew to a narrow agenda. Issues allowed for discussion run the gamut, from A to...B. The talking heads on TV are Washington courtiers reminiscent of sycophants in a monarch's court. At best, debate on these talk shows is establishmentarian, with a dreary balance between pro and con, between Democrat and Republican, between tweedle-dum and tweedle-dee. At worst, these shows are shills and press agents for the administration in power and serve to disseminate the pre-existing "talking points" from political party headquarters. The bias isn't toward any ideology — it's toward officialdom. Add the influence of our short-attention span entertainment culture, and it's no wonder that the national debate has become a petty shouting match among partisans.

In a city where credentials provide entrée, former government officials easily find second life as pundits. It's fairly easy to get a seat on the Sunday talk shows if you once worked in a presidential administration and you can speak in snappy slogans. The key distinction: get the attention of the gatekeepers who book the appointments. Arguably the best way to get their attention is to stick to Business-to-Business topics. Go after the B-to-B niche shows, because they have the widest appeal.

Don't be overly impressed by the blustering bloviators you see on television every Sunday morning. There was a time when punditry was a mere ancillary to journalism. An opinion column was awarded to long-time newspapermen (and they were almost always men) as a reward for years of hard work. Legends such as Walter Lippmann earned their spurs before they influenced public opinion and presidents. Now, punditry is available to any self-infatuated schmuck with a slick resume, a baritone voice, a dark suit and a clever pitch.

THE CONFESSIONS OF AN INK-STAINED WRETCH

Many panelists are only nominal journalists with puffed-up titles. There is no significant bar to entry, no minimum experience required — and no code of ethics. In a famous example of conflict of interest, über-pundit George Will once helped prep Ronald Reagan before a presidential debate — and then went on the tube to breathlessly opine about Reagan's superlative showing. Will, a bow-tied Tory, never subscribed to H.L. Mencken's wise dictum: "The only way for a reporter to look at a politician is down." But then again, Will has never been a reporter.

Personal opinion and television production values have merged to form a mutant form of journalism that, it can be argued, is harming democracy. But as a marketer, you shouldn't care about all that stuff from civics class. What matters is that you become a player. As the opium-enhanced Samuel Coleridge wrote in his epic poem, *The Rime of the Ancient Mariner:* "A thousand thousand slimy things lived on, and so did I."

If they play their cards right, TV and radio pundits become entrepreneurs who capitalize on their fame to write bestselling books and rake in huge lecture fees. Punditry has become a lucrative cottage industry — journalists have evolved from "muckrakers" to "buckrakers." Think of it as a form of white-collar crime.

Truth is no obstacle to opinion. Indeed, it's staggering the amount of outright lies, disinformation, agitprop and spin that's prevalent on news talk shows. If you have a self-interested message to trumpet, don't be shy. As I've made clear in previous chapters, television has killed reality. More to the point, the line between "fact" and "opinion" has been irrevocably blurred.

CHAPTER 5: THE RISE OF THE PUNDITOCRACY

You don't need to be an intellectual or even particularly bright to get invited to a talk show, but it's still not easy. As with everything else it touches, television has coarsened and vulgarized the quality of discourse. The triviality, if not sheer inanity of TV debate, will often stoop to the level of an average network sitcom.

But take note: a new and unstoppable media force may be making TV and radio punditry obsolete — as I will explain in Chapter Seven. For now, let's look at how to survive a journalistic interview, and turn a dangerous situation into one that actually works to your advantage.

Chapter 6

OPEN MOUTH, EXTRACT FOOT

How to Survive a Press Interview

Richelieu, the Machiavellian Prime Minister of King Louis XIII, was in many ways the precursor to folks like Karl Rove. But to be fair, journalists don't play nice, either. Many of them derive sadistic pleasure from making their interview subject squirm. They're not above sandbagging their interviewee with an unexpected and sensitive question, just to make him or her sweat.

> "IF YOU GIVE ME SIX LINES WRITTEN BY THE HAND OF THE MOST HONEST OF MEN, I WILL FIND SOMETHING IN THEM WHICH WILL HANG HIM."
> – Cardinal Richelieu

THE CONFESSIONS OF AN INK-STAINED WRETCH

> Journalists come into an interview with their own preconceived agenda. All too often, they've already written the interview in their heads, before they've even asked a question. Journalists tend to be lazy and run in safe packs, but at the same time, they covet a reputation for being tough, adversarial and muckracking. It adds up to cheap shots.

This chapter will show you how to prepare yourself — or your client — for media interviews.

Over the years, I've conducted countless interviews with top corporate CEOs and powerful politicians. My interviews have graced the covers of major magazines and the front pages of large circulation newspapers. These interviews took place in a multitude of locations — over breakfast, dinner or lunch; in the person's office; in a cafeteria, restaurant or factory floor; in an airplane; or — when I served as editor-in-chief of *Rotor & Wing* magazine — while at the controls of a helicopter. I'm not a licensed pilot, but I racked up many hours of "stick time" while questioning aerospace CEOs.

As a reporter, I liked to put the executive in a setting that made him or her comfortable. This setting also provided colorful context material that I would weave into the article. But I had another agenda, as well: the more comfortable the interviewee, the more likely you can extract valuable and closely held information. That's especially true over a long

CHAPTER 6: OPEN MOUTH, EXTRACT FOOT

dinner, where the conversation is on the record and alcohol is being served. I'd start with softball questions, earn their trust, get them relaxed, tell a few jokes, cover ground that they enjoyed, and then, slowly but surely, my questions would get tougher and tougher. The technique is similar to slowly tightening a net around your prey.

Another favored tactic of mine is to put my notebook into my breast pocket and then ask a tough question — while still on the record. As I listen to the answer, I won't take notes. The subconscious message is: "This is just between you and me." But in fact, the rules of the interview were never changed.

Then, a few minutes later, like Michael Corleone in the famous restaurant scene, I announce that I must go to the bathroom. In the men's room stall, I furiously write down the answers from memory. When I return, I don't shoot my interviewee in the head with a gun — but the effect is metaphorically the same. Be forewarned: I'm not the first guy to come up with these tactics.

Joseph Kennedy, the patriarch of the Kennedy political dynasty, once said: "It's not who you actually are that counts, but who people think you are." The public only knows about people what they learn in the media. Many powerful celebrities have been ruined, or permanently sullied, by ill-advised remarks during an interview. I'll never forget watching one of my cinematic heroes, Sean Connery, inform Barbara Walters during a television interview that it's okay to hit women — that smacking a woman was sometimes the only appropriate way to handle her. Walters was visibly taken aback as one of the world's biggest movie stars condoned violence against women. The man who played the definitive James Bond came across as a chauvinistic boor, and he never quite lived it down with his fans.

THE CONFESSIONS OF AN INK-STAINED WRETCH

```
As a reporter, I liked to put the
executive in a setting that made him
or her comfortable. This setting also
provided colorful context material
that I would weave into the article.
But I had another agenda: the more
comfortable the interviewee, the more
likely you can extract closely held
information.
```

BEWARE OF CHEAP SHOTS

Journalists come into an interview with their own preconceived agenda. All too often, they've already written the interview in their heads, before they've even asked a question. Journalists tend to be lazy and run in safe packs, but at the same time, they covet a reputation for being tough, adversarial and muckraking. It adds up to cheap shots. Brace yourself for no-win questions, along the lines of the old Groucho Marx joke: "When did you stop beating your wife?" On page 111 are my 10 tips for preparing for a media interview.

In most cases, my interviewees over the years have been shrewd enough to avoid pissing me off. They've followed these 10 rules and by doing so, done themselves a big favor. But occasionally, I've interviewed people who are shockingly clueless. These people could have benefited from this book.

One aerospace CEO in particular (who shall remain nameless) would repeatedly get flustered, even though I emailed him a list of talking points in advance. I even included on my list a few of his suggested questions — he proferred only sotfballs, of course. I'd ask a fairly

CHAPTER 6: OPEN MOUTH, EXTRACT FOOT

innocuous question and he'd imperiously point at my tape recorder and bark: "Turn that thing off!" Then after gathering his thoughts, he'd command: "Okay, turn it back on." Then he would give me a lame, milquetoast answer that was useless corporate-speak. After the interview, he demanded to see my notes before we published the Q&A in my magazine. I refused. He put up a stink and threatened to call my publisher. I didn't back down and his threat proved a bluff.

The upshot? I developed a deep dislike for this pompous clown. In the end, the interview came out okay and I was objective. The final article itself was fine. However, behind the scenes, I silently vowed to never interview him again. I added his name to my internal "blacklist" of assholes. While his competitors were getting ink, he was relegated to no-man's-land.

Many journalists harbor such a blacklist. You never, ever want yourself or your client to make it to this list. If you follow my 10 tips for surviving a media interview, you won't.

TEN TIPS FOR SURVIVING A MEDIA INTERVIEW

Before you meet a journalist from any type of medium for a major one-on-one interview, read and internalize these proven tips:

1. ASK THE REPORTER FOR A LIST OF TALKING POINTS IN ADVANCE

Journalists are touchy about giving out the questions in advance, but you will probably succeed if you ask for a general list of "talking points" before the interview. Make the argument that you want to do your homework before the interview, to ensure that your answers are as thoughtful and substantive as possible. Acknowledge the reporter's right to ask whatever he, or she, wants. But ask for talking points, with the rationale that getting at least a few general questions in advance will make it a better interview and increase the odds of success. You

THE CONFESSIONS OF AN INK-STAINED WRETCH

want to make your media friend look good by raising the quality of the interview.

2. PREPARE YOUR OWN TALKING POINTS
■ Regardless of what the journalist sends you, supplement the list with your own. Think through the message you want to convey. What's your marketing goal in this interview? Practice and "role play" with a colleague. If you just breeze into the interview unprepared, you will be sorry later.

3. NEVER LIE
■ It seems odd to recommend total honesty, when politicians of all persuasions lie all the time and often get away with it. But they're experienced and polished prevaricators. More to the point, they sometimes get caught, usually with adverse consequences. If a journalist catches you in a lie, you're sunk. They'll put your severed head on a pike and subject you to public shame. The media crows will come to peck out your lifeless eyes. You'll never be trusted again.

4. INCLUDE INTERESTING PERSONAL ANECDOTES
■ Try to be charming, without being smarmy. You don't have to act like a toothy game show host, but try to weave into your remarks a few personal details, for humor and color. These anecdotes will humanize you, with the journalist and the public.

5. KEEP YOUR ANSWERS CONCISE
■ Resist the urge to pontificate. Answer the question succinctly and then move on. Journalists get testy when you start to put them to sleep. They might ask you a nasty question, just out of spite for being bored.

CHAPTER 6: OPEN MOUTH, EXTRACT FOOT

6. WRITE, MEMORIZE AND PRACTICE A FEW TRANSITIONAL SENTENCES

If you watch or read an interview with a politician or business leader, you'll notice the graceful ease with which they can deflect tough questions or change the subject. It often boils down to the right segue. For example, if you're suddenly confronted with an awkward question that you really don't want to answer, you can say: "Great question! I'm glad you asked that." Then, segue to an anecdote or tangential issue that subtly changes the subject.

For example:
Q: "Why did your campaign deploy dirty tricks against your opponent? Your charges against him have since been proven false."

A: "I'm glad you broached the subject of negative campaigning. Americans are sick-and-tired of the politics of destruction. That's why I've called for tighter restrictions on Political Action Committees and 527 groups. Next question."

7. USE THE INTERVIEWER'S FIRST NAME; MAKE SMALL TALK BEFORE THE INTERVIEW

Before the interview, try to be a mensch. If a holiday is close on the calendar, ask about the interviewer's plans. Swap stories about your kids. Don't overdo it and lapse into obsequiousness — that would backfire on you. But connect with the interviewer first. You'll be treated better if they see you as a human being and not just an abstraction. Instead of "industry tycoon" or "elected official," you'll maybe become a person they don't want to mistreat.

My favorite story of how this aspect was famously mishandled goes back to David Frost's television interviews with Richard Nixon, after Nixon had resigned in disgrace. Before the cameras started rolling,

THE CONFESSIONS OF AN INK-STAINED WRETCH

Nixon made a characteristically maladroit attempt at male bonding with Frost. While riding in an elevator with his interviewer, Nixon tried to break the ice by asking Sir David: "So, David. Did you do any fornicating over the weekend?"

8. GET TO KNOW THE OUTLET AHEAD OF TIME

As with all of your press releases and marketing collateral, you must tailor your message and remarks to the focus and "beat" of the media outlet that is interviewing you. Get copies of previous interviews, to learn the substance, tone and style of their interviews. Learn more about their audience and the subject matter that tends to get explored. If you demonstrate this knowledge during the interview, the journalist will love you for it. You'll have earned respect and your questions will be more substantive.

You don't want to merely survive the interview — you also want to hit it out of the park. A media interview is an opportunity that you should exploit to its fullest. The better your answers, the more likely that it will end up on the front page of, say, the business section of the newspaper, or better still, as a cover story for a magazine.

9. OFFER ASSISTANCE

Whenever I served as editor of a magazine, my art budget was always limited. I had to be resourceful when it came to photography and graphical supports. Whenever I interviewed a top executive, the really savvy ones would put expensive photographers at my disposal, paid for by their company. There's nothing unethical in this. The result would be great photos, art directed by myself. This logistical assistance increased the odds that the interview would end up on the cover of my magazine.

CHAPTER 6: OPEN MOUTH, EXTRACT FOOT

TOP THREE INTERVIEW "NO-NO'S"

These three common interview blunders are as insidious — and deadly — as a Viet Cong boobytrap. Make sure you or your client avoids stepping into them:

1. CONFUSING AN INTERVIEW WITH AN INTERROGATION

Unless Mike Wallace and a camera crew from "60 Minutes" suddenly enter the room, don't get defensive. Sure, danger lurks in any interview. But more likely than not, the purpose of the interview isn't to subject the interviewee to a full-scale Gestapo grilling.

2. LETTING YOUR CELL PHONE RING

Sounds obvious, but I can't tell you how many times a self-important and careless executive has left his cell phone on during an interview. It conveys a lack of respect and really pisses off the interviewer. Don't be a putz. Turn off your cell phone.

3. MAKING A DIRTY JOKE

Journalists tend to be an irreverent bunch. But you know what? Our esteemed profession is getting more corporate and conformist, with each passing day. The interviewee can really embarrass himself, and cast a pall over the rest of the interview, by attempting too much levity and making off-color remarks. I've seen it happen, and it's painful to watch.

If asked to sit for an interview, offer similar assistance. Chances are, the journalist is constrained by a limited budget. Offer the services of a transcriber, perhaps one who works internally in your organization, to quickly turn the tape recordings into electronic transcripts. Again, the journalist will love you for it.

THE CONFESSIONS OF AN INK-STAINED WRETCH

```
It seems odd to recommend total hon-
esty, when politicians of all persua-
sions lie all the time and often get
away with it. But they're polished
prevaricators. More to the point, they
sometimes get caught, usually with
adverse consequences. If a journalist
catches you in a lie, you're sunk.
```

10. CONTROL YOUR EMOTIONS

■ Never get visibly flustered. Don't get angry. If you feel annoyance rising inside of you, don't indulge it. Stay cool, baby. If the journalist starts to piss you off, then follow the example of the android Commander Data in Star Trek: disconnect your emotion chip. Nothing will sink you faster than getting testy or snippy with the reporter. It's like arguing with a cop over a speeding ticket. Challenge the reporter's ego and you're gonna lose, big time.

Journalists can use the First Amendment as a club to mercilessly beat those they dislike. They'll deny it, of course, but they're subject to petty human emotions, just like everyone else. If you challenge a reporter's ego, if you embarrass or threaten a reporter during an interview, you will pay. Make a little joke at their expense and they'll get even with you where it hurts — within the published interview.

Sometimes, during an interview, an overbearing CEO will make an aside that infuriates me, and it takes all of the self-discipline I can

CHAPTER 6: OPEN MOUTH, EXTRACT FOOT

muster to not screw the interviewee in print. Not all reporters are as fair-minded as yours truly.

WAGE SLAVES IN THE WORD FACTORY

If you perform the duties of an editorial assistant for your media contact, they will seek you out over and over again, because you will have gained a reputation as someone easy to work with. If you assist them often enough, you will become virtually indispensable and, eventually, you will have them wrapped around your finger.

Editors typically don't have secretaries or administrative assistants. Most publications, for example, have severely downsized to the point where almost no one has a secretary. This is even more true today than it was 10 years ago, as publishers now have to compete with all the free content that is available on the Internet.

You'd be surprised how many newspapers and magazines run on shoestring budgets — I call them "bring-your-own-pen" operations. That's especially true of newsletter companies, which tend to be sweatshops. I once worked for a newsletter company in which all employees sat in an "open office" that lacked even the most basic cubicle walls. Pay was low and the workload, onerous. Creative people were expected to function inside a goldfish bowl. That's why the motto of journalism should be the inverse of the old Army slogan: "It's not an adventure. It's just a job."

As I said previously, shoulder a little extra work and give the hard-pressed editor some backup assistance. Your investment of time and effort will reap plenty of dividends down the road.

THE CONFESSIONS OF AN INK-STAINED WRETCH

Some marketers are hesitant to aggressively offer such help to the media, for fear of "stepping on toes." It's true that you must respect the purview of the journalist. But if you've learned anything by now, you'll understand that most journalists are overworked and stressed out, and they seek whatever assistance they can muster. Without being too pushy or (heaven forbid) condescending, make yourself an informal partner of the journalist — in this case, the interviewer. If your client is scheduled or is lobbying for an interview, create a rough script and offer it to your media contact. It will work wonders.

Getting the script ahead of time increases their comfort level, conveys a sense of professionalism and makes them more cooperative during the interview. The script serves as parameters for the interview; within those parameters, both parties will extemporize, to lend the interview an impression of spontaneity. Not all journalists bother to prepare; many are happy to just "wing it." That's why you can get a leg up, by doing the preparation for them.

Our next chapter is perhaps the most important in the book. We'll look at the dramatic changes the press has undergone in the last 10 years, and how you can adapt these time-honored tactics to the new environment of bloggers and podcasters.

Chapter 7

BARBARIANS AT THE GATE

In This Brave New World, YOU are The Media

Reading Ken Olson's staggeringly obtuse prediction brings to mind another famous quote, from the Duff-quaffing philosopher Homer Simpson: "D'oh!"

But the personal computer has been here a long time, and it has revolutionized our lives in ways that even the most far-sighted visionaries of 1977 could not have predicted.

> **"THERE IS NO REASON ANYONE WOULD WANT A COMPUTER IN THEIR HOME."**
> – Ken Olson, founder, Digital Equipment Corp., speaking in 1977.

Had I been writing this book 25 years ago, it would have been solely about how you could influence that handful of editors and producers who acted as "gatekeepers" of the information needed by America's top corporations and government officials.

THE CONFESSIONS OF AN INK-STAINED WRETCH

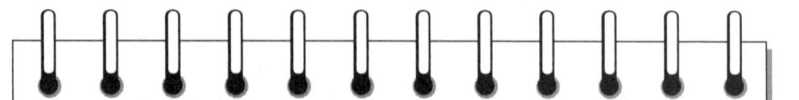

> Don't make your audience think. Get their attention immediately. Make matters clear, apparent, compelling and do so instantly. Society isn't merely molded by television anymore; it's molded by the "quick-cut" editing of MTV and video games.

But today those gatekeepers are the ones on the defensive. I just read that the market value of Google, the Internet search engine that didn't exist 10 years ago, is now more than 10 times the value of *The New York Times*, the world's leading newspaper.

One financial expert quoted in the piece said that "in another couple of years, the youngsters won't even know that *The New York Times* exists as anything but private-label news source for an Internet portal." Wow!

So if you want to get your message out, it's not enough to know your way around the established media (although that's still an essential element of a comprehensive strategy). You need to remember that in this brave new world, YOU are the media. Instead of trying to get press from journalists, you can *become* the journalist, by creating your own blog or podcast.

Not just content is affected. As a famous Canadian thinker once said: "The medium is the message." (No, not William Shatner — I'm referring to Marshall McLuhan.) McLuhan postulated that image-based

CHAPTER 7: BARBARIANS AT THE GATE

media, e.g., television, is passive and emotional in nature — it bypasses linear, analytical logic and goes right to your subjective emotions. That's why presidential elections are hugely influenced by 30-second attack ads on TV.

So what does it all add up to? From your perspective as a marketer, it means: *don't make your audience think*. Get their attention immediately. Make matters clear, apparent, compelling and do so instantly. Society isn't merely molded by television anymore; it's molded by the "quick-cut" editing of MTV and video games. This split-second sensibility pervades all aspects of our culture. The time you have to capture someone's interest is measured by the time it takes an electrical impulse to flash across a synapse. If your lede is muddy or unclear and it makes the reader scratch his head — zip! He's gone. His attention has been stolen by the multitude of other media competing for his truncated attention span.

The Internet has made news intraday, instantaneous and accessible to all. The Internet's profound transformation of daily life is especially acute for journalists. As the great press curmudgeon A. J. Liebling put it: "Power of the press belongs to those who own a press." With the advent of the Internet, now everyone owns one.

On the Internet, data continually pours forth like water out of a pressurized water hose. Many digital pundits pronounce that "print is dead", and that the Internet will completely replace printed media. On the contrary, the Wild West of the Internet makes the quality press — the mainstream metro daily broadsheets and the old-fashioned ink-stained wretches of the newsroom — even more important. They make sense of the informational chaos and they function as molders of elite opinion.

So, let's debunk a big myth, right now. Print is not dead.

www.inkstainedconfessions.com

THE CONFESSIONS OF AN INK-STAINED WRETCH

That said, journalists must swim in the same digital ocean as the rest of us. The Internet has completely changed their organizations and their daily functioning as reporters. Rather than gathering information by applying shoe leather to the pavement or hitting the telephone, reporters increasingly sit in their cubicles and simply use Google.

THE RISE OF MULTIMEDIA JOURNALISM
In the grand sweep of communications history, the emergence of new media has never completely obliterated the existing technologies. Instead, the modes of production fall by the wayside. Linotype printing presses and typewriters became obsolete, not the written journalistic word. Radio didn't destroy newspapers, and television didn't destroy radio. All of these media evolved to accommodate each other. The same dynamic holds true for the Internet and its stepchildren, the bloggers and podcasters.

And yet, despite this broadening of journalistic sources and options, your task as a marketer — to get ink (and bandwidth!) for your message — is just as difficult as ever. Less than 10 percent of the news that's disseminated by the wire services (e.g., Associated Press and Reuters) and other centralized news agencies gets picked up by newspapers, television and radio. Further research shows that people remember only about 10 percent of the news that they read, see or hear.

What you must consider is how the Internet has altered the relationship between journalists and their audience. Consumers of news can now take ownership of how they want to receive news. RSS feeds and aggregators have changed all modes of communication. Readers can skip from one archived document to another, thereby fracturing time and space. People still read, but not necessarily in a linear fashion. Getting news from one source is antiquated. With the Internet, consumers of news can chose from a smorgasbord composed of the

CHAPTER 7: BARBARIANS AT THE GATE

Internet, newspapers, magazines, radio, television, wire services, archives, bloggers and podcasters.

The rise of the Internet, along with related developments like the hundreds of cable TV channels now available, has made it possible to reach niche audiences much more effectively than in the days of the old, broad-based media. The key step is determining which niche contains your target market, and which sites serve that niche. And remember: you can directly serve that niche yourself — or work collaboratively with other sites.

The "Five Ws" and the "inverted pyramid," as explained in earlier chapters, should still govern your writing. These rules are timeless. But you must also take into account the fact that your reader is bound to take several hyperlinked detours along the way. The age of "www" has ushered in the age of ADD — Attention Deficit Disorder. Creating, accessing and distributing news has become extremely complex. Witness the emergence of bloggers and podcasters (see sidebar, page 128).

Orville Schell, dean of the University of California at Berkeley's journalism school, recently told *BusinessWeek* magazine: "The Roman Empire that was mass media is breaking up, and we are entering an almost-feudal period where there will be many more centers of power and influence."

If the mass media is the Roman Empire, then bloggers, podcasters and other guerilla journalists — and those of you who will aggressively use the new technologies to get your message out — are the barbarians at the gates.

Another, rather more flattering, analogy for these 21st century messengers is that they're David taking on Goliath. In fact, Glenn Reynolds,

THE CONFESSIONS OF AN INK-STAINED WRETCH

who runs the popular political blog Instapundit, recently published a book on this theme called *An Army of Davids*. The proliferation of viewpoints on the Internet can often advance the dialogue faster than a handful of self-appointed experts, much as the thousands of participants in an economic market can make the best choice about which products are the best. To be sure, *An Army of Davids* is taking on the corporate Goliath.

This rising challenge to the media oligarchy is a heartening development, but we haven't entered Utopia just yet. Authoritarian governments are making a rear guard action against the Internet, with the aim of curtailing its freedom.

One notable example is the successful efforts of the Chinese authorities to censor the Internet. It remains to be seen how these efforts pan out (some are already referring to the "Great Firewall of China"). I remain hopeful that they are doomed to fail. Information wants to be free.

Influencing bloggers is trickier than influencing their mainstream counterparts. The contempt and low regard that journalists harbor for marketers and PR people is greatly magnified among bloggers, who tend to be fiercely dogmatic about their independence.

Bloggers are clamoring to influence the media and become integral to it, but at the same time they disdain the established media and they draw their identities and energy through their opposition to it.

Bloggers tend to be "bourgeois bohemians" who want it both ways, and as such, they suffer from cognitive dissonance. They want a seat at the media table, but they simultaneously want to turn the table over and smash it to bits. And they've scored some notable successes, as when they challenged the authenticity of those documents relating to

CHAPTER 7: BARBARIANS AT THE GATE

President Bush's National Guard service, essentially forcing Dan Rather, a giant of the Old Media, into early retirement.

Michael Barone, editor of the widely used *Almanac of American Politics*, wrote recently that when he started covering politics in the 1970s, you could cover a presidential campaign by knowing what went on in five rooms: the headquarters of the two campaigns and the conference rooms of the three major television networks. But in the 21st century, the power is much more widely diffused throughout our society.

You can use this dynamic to your advantage. Here's how.

RSS — REAL SIMPLE SYNDICATION

To get your own message out on the Internet without any middlemen, you need to understand RSS. You may have seen this acronym at various web sites you may have visited. But if you intend to build your own site or use the Internet to cut out the various media middlemen, you need to understand what it's all about.

RSS is a family of XML file formats for Web syndication. Some say the acronym stands for Rich Site Summary, others Real Simple Syndication. RSS technology enables subscriptions to web sites that have provided RSS feeds; these are typically sites that continually change or add content.

RSS is a standard for publishing regular updates to web-based content. Using this standard, Web publishers provide updates, such as the latest news headlines or weblog postings. Meanwhile, consumers use RSS reader applications — or one of a growing number of online services — to collect and monitor their favorite feeds in one place (RSS content from a publisher, viewed in one of these readers, is often called a

THE CONFESSIONS OF AN INK-STAINED WRETCH

BLOGGERS AND PODCASTERS

Blogging (an abbreviated evolution of the term "weblog") is a personal web page with continually updated material that melds the quotidian details of the blogger's personal or professional life with what is happening in a given market or subject area. Or, the blog is just informational. There are as many types of blogs as there are individuals who create them. Opinionated, computer-savvy iconoclasts were operating blogs before the term became a hot buzzword, but the trend accelerated into popular consciousness with the advent of automated, cheap and easy-to-use publishing systems, notably "Blogger" at blogger.com.

Three big developments catapulted blogs into the news mainstream: the debunking of Dan Rather's facts, in his aforementioned *60 Minutes* story about President Bush's checkered National Guard record; the spotlight on U.S. Sen. Trent Lott's racially insensitive remarks at U.S. Sen. Strom Thurmond's birthday party, leading to Lott's removal as Majority Leader; and the lending of news cycle longevity (or "legs") to the Swift Boat Veterans for Truth attack on U.S. Sen. John Kerry.

The emergence of blogs has democratized and fragmented the news process, especially in the realm of politics. Now, all you need is a laptop and broadband access, and you can park yourself at a political event and become a player, alongside *The New York Times* and *The Washington Post*. Bloggers aren't part of the pack — not yet, anyway. They break stories the rest of the media ignore; they influence debate, they act as gadflies, they wheedle and cajole, they're uninhibited and the mainstream media doesn't quite know what to make of them. But they're here to stay, and they can serve as powerful tools in your marketing arsenal.

CHAPTER 7: BARBARIANS AT THE GATE

> **Podcasting** (combining the words "broadcasting" with "iPod") is a method of distributing audio programs over the Internet, enabling listeners to subscribe and get new shows downloaded onto their computer or mp3 player, as they're released. Podcasting differs from similar types of online media delivery because it's based on a subscription model, which uses a feed (such as RSS) to deliver an audio file. Podcasting allows unaffiliated producers to generate their own syndicated "radio" and "television" shows; it also provides established broadcast radio stations a new method to distribute content. The term "podcast" is a misnomer because neither podcasting nor listening to podcasts requires an iPod.
>
> Podcasting is exploding in popularity. As of Nov. 2005, 70 percent of podcast listeners access programs on their computers, not through MP3 players. Lengths vary, but a typical podcast can last anywhere from 10 to 30 minutes. Any software that can play a sound file can play a podcast. Podcasts can very easily take the format of a news interview; that's why marketers should think of podcasts as yet another vehicle for promoting their message (see sidebar, page 136). For a list of various podcast directories, to which you can add your own podcast: http://www.podcastingnews.com/topics/Podcast_Directory.html.

"feed"). Notable examples include www.NewsGator.com, www.FeedDemon.com or www.Bloglines.com (for a complete list, go to www.inkstainedconfessions.com).

To deploy this technology, users must set up an aggregation service, which is akin to a mailbox.

What does RSS mean for publishers of information? It permits instant distribution of content updates to consumers. What does it mean for consumers of information? RSS makes it possible to review a large number of sites in a very short time.

THE CONFESSIONS OF AN INK-STAINED WRETCH

> People still read, but not necessarily in a linear fashion. Getting news from one source is antiquated. With the Internet, consumers of news can chose from a smorgasbord composed of the Internet, newspapers, magazines, radio, television, wire services, archives, bloggers and podcasters.

How can you publish your own RSS feed? If you have a web site, weblog or podcast — and if you don't, you need one — you can add RSS syndication as a publishing option, in some cases automatically. How easy this is to accomplish depends on how your site is served today. If you are using a hosted publishing tool like TypePad or Blogger, you probably publish a feed automatically. Investigate whether your provider's administration tools offer feed-related options or controls. Other types of web sites and application platforms may require some programming skills in order to add RSS syndication capabilities. Free software tools are available to generate your own RSS feeds (again, consult my web site for links).

RSS is almost a mainstream technology; consumer services are rapidly moving to integrate it into existing products. And that's just for bringing the reader the latest headlines, personal publications and other textual content.

The next frontier for RSS is facilitating client communication. For example, a company called Basecamp (www.basecamphq.com) offers a web-based project management tool that allows you to monitor the lat-

CHAPTER 7: BARBARIANS AT THE GATE

est updates, communications, deadlines and other activities across your internal and client projects via RSS. There are other companies that offer similar services; check them out and see which one is right for your needs.

For a complete tutorial on RSS: http://www.mnot.net/RSS/tutorial/

THE EFFICACY OF ONLINE COMMUNICATIONS

All of these "New Media" niches combined reach a cumulatively larger audience than the Old Media. Here's a look at what's available.

Certain companies (notably Macromedia and WebEx) can help you create and operate webcasts that supplement your press releases and conferences. Increasing numbers of marketers and PR professionals are discovering the practical and very tangible benefits of web-based communications.

Webcasts can make your promotional efforts more efficient, cost-effective and persuasive. You can create a webcast predicated on your press release or marketing collateral, and then insert the URL for that webcast high up in your written piece. The webcast will serve as a force-multiplier for your print-based message. You can do the same with podcasts and blogs. The three leaders in this space are WebEx, Macromedia's Breeze and Microsoft's Live Meeting.

Online presentations represent the leading edge in communications, but at the same time, the upfront capital expenditures are small. Without costly investments in additional computer equipment and software, online communications allow marketers to quickly communicate — visually, aurally and compellingly — with journalists. Also keep in mind, you can send recorded audio information and commentary to

www.inkstainedconfessions.com

THE CONFESSIONS OF AN INK-STAINED WRETCH

other podcasters, who will in turn serve as marketers for you, by disseminating your "clip". (For more information on viral marketing through podcasts, go to www.inkstainedconfessions.com.)

We're all trained to look at a screen nowadays, whether it's a television or a computer. Our brains have become hard-wired to expect visual components to all messages. That's how online communications can help you, without sacrificing the essential component of the written word.

Webcasts typically use PowerPoints as their foundation, allowing marketers the flexibility to adopt existing content and easily add sound, charts, graphs, screen shots and animations. Web-based, on-demand presentations give marketers a powerful new tool in their arsenal. However, don't fall into the common pitfall of merely focusing on online media, just to show the press that you're cool, hip and Internet-savvy. Don't use technology for its own sake; it's a means to an end, not the end in itself. Online communications should enhance — not replace — existing print media efforts. Important functions, such as the need in key situations for personalized contact, are not eliminated.

Web-based marketing doesn't preclude the need to talk to journalists. Exploiting the "New Media" of the Internet doesn't replace the tried-and-true techniques of sending hard copy press releases, making follow-up phone calls and holding live in-person press conferences. Webcasts, podcasts and the like should be used to augment your existing efforts, to make them more robust, compelling and persuasive.

Savvy marketers are using online media to supplement in-person meetings with reporters and editors. These meetings remain crucial. That said, let's not diminish the important leverage provided by on-demand online presentations. Marketers can easily use webcast programs to

CHAPTER 7: BARBARIANS AT THE GATE

convert their PowerPoint presentations into narrated, multimedia presentations that journalists can view at their convenience.

New webcast technologies allow marketers to quickly forge creative promotional presentations in PowerPoint, without special training or technical assistance. To boost the effect of on-demand presentations, they can even record narration and synchronize it with animations. They can add audio recording, quiz creation and publishing wizards within familiar PowerPoint menus.

You can become your own impresario of audio-enhanced presentations. Available webcast technology allows flexible on-demand delivery of marketing pitches through any standard browser. By using on-demand presentations, a marketer doesn't need to be a multimedia "expert" to quickly and easily create slick, high-quality multimedia presentations. What's more, journalists can easily view these presentations 24/7.

The popularity of online communication methods, and their growing influence within all media, is in large measure a function of the pervasiveness of the Internet. Increasingly, people have broadband access in the workplace. The Internet is ubiquitous, in the office and at home. Consequently, journalists don't simply want access to information — they want to be able to immediately use that information. It behooves you to deliver the right information to the right journalists, just in time, so they can do something with the information. That's why marketers must utilize web-based media, to give their media prospects instantaneous access to breaking, up-to-the-second information.

The typical journalist requires — no, he craves with every fiber of his being — unimpeded access to real-time data. Your role is to place streams of real-time data (otherwise known as "breaking news") into context for the journalist, to provide an analytical overlay that distin-

THE CONFESSIONS OF AN INK-STAINED WRETCH

WRITING FOR THE INTERNET

Most of the rules cited in this book are universal and timeless. They have long applied to all types of writing, and they always will. However, reading from a computer screen is different than reading from paper. Studies have shown that reading online is about 25 percent slower than reading from print. Most online readers aren't reading; they're scanning. If writing for a web site, here are a few special pointers:

» Immediately clobber your reader over the head with your main points, at the top of the web page.

» Use lots of subheads and bullets — even more than you would for a print document. A gray wall of type turns off print readers and it's especially deadly for typically impatient online readers.

» Write brief paragraphs that are separated by a blank line. White space makes web display easier and more compelling to read. It also reduces eyestrain.

guishes mere data from insight. Part and parcel of this insight, of course, is the message you're selling.

By using the online tools described in this chapter, you allow journalistic prospects to see and hear information from their desktops or from remote peripheral devices, making your marketing pitch a richer, and more interactive experience.

Online communications expedite the extremely fast dissemination of essential information — what Internet wonks call "rapid knowledge transfer." For example, you can use online methods to quickly tell

CHAPTER 7: BARBARIANS AT THE GATE

> » Use short sentences; avoid compound sentences with lots of clauses. Stick to simple, active construction: subject, verb and object. For example: "Spot catches the ball."
>
> » Use the present tense as much as possible.
>
> » The Web is conversational, intimate and friendly. Use "we" and "you." Write as if the words are part of a dinner conversation with an old friend. Be chatty.
>
> » In emails, concisely but completely describe the content of your message in the subject header.
>
> » Set your margins for a hard return after every 65 characters, to ensure short lines that can be read at a glance.
>
> » Use contractions (won't, I'll, etc.). You want your writing to require as little effort to read as possible.

journalists about a breaking news event. You may not have the time to thoroughly brief them on the event, but you can grab their attention and make them grateful for your intercession by getting the information to them as it's unfolding — and by being first with the news. Journalists love scoops. Most of them are shameless little beasts that would unhook their grandmother's respirator tube to get a front-page story.

Your goal is to reach a broad number of journalists, but with a high-impact and creative message. Online media, particularly on-demand webcasts, convey a rich media experience on a broad level that doesn't require sophisticated expertise to create. Marketers can then tie-in their presentation through an email hot link or web site. As I mention

THE CONFESSIONS OF AN INK-STAINED WRETCH

PODCASTS: A TRANSFORMATIVE TECHNOLOGY

Podcasts represent a "disruptive technology" that is revolutionizing communications, just as Gutenberg's printing press in the 15th century revolutionized communications and society, by putting media and media production into the hands of the masses.

Keep in mind, though, that podcasts are not a replacement for existing marketing and promotional efforts — they complement and serve as an adjunct to your traditional approaches (e.g., press releases and press conferences).

Conducting a press conference? Record it and then make the mp3 available at a hot link that is emailed to reporters. Or, when disseminating a press release, incorporate URLs in the body of the copy that lead readers to podcasts that convey helpful background information. Better yet, be part of the communication. Make yourself an expert with your own online forum.

Podcasts put the entire control of informational access into the palms of listeners' hands. Podcasts take your existing marketing message and make it faster, more efficient and more intimate. A major strength of podcasts is that they're permission based. The audience spends more time with podcasts than with conventional ads.

Podcasts aren't merely a novelty or a technological bell and whistle. They're increasingly "mainstream" and, as such, you need to use them to get the media's attention. Indeed, the new Oxford American Dictionary named "Podcast" as the new "Word of the Year" for 2005. Podcasts can be customized, so they're always relevant to any audience. It's a dialogue — not a monologue — that has great appeal for listeners because they control when (and whether) to hear it.

CHAPTER 7: BARBARIANS AT THE GATE

As I've pointed out earlier in this book, today's hyperlinked 24/7 economy has turned markets into conversations, conducted in a human voice. They're no longer a top-down monologue. Put podcasts into your marketing mix, and your communications will be immediate, relevant and in a human voice that's genuine and persuasive. And remember, you can wring promotion from existing podcasters, by sending them clips of your work.

Podcasts allow you to increase and intensify the frequency of your message. Podcasting works best as a marketing tool that communicates, educates and drives listeners to action in situations when you need to intensify the frequency and intimacy of the message. The listener has the ability to say yes or no, to subscribe or not subscribe. Podcasts are a qualitatively higher experience, because they're so thoroughly permission-based.

For more detailed information on podcasts, I highly recommend Larstan's series of books on podcasting: "Podcasting 101," "Promoting Your Podcast," and "Business Podcasting" (http://www.PodcastingUniversity.org). All edited by yours truly, these books explain the nitty-gritty, how-to details of successfully using podcasts as a marketing and communications tool.

above, one effective method is to set up a webcast that's relevant to your message, and then insert a URL "call to action" within the press release that is an invitation to attend a webcast (sometimes called a "webinar"). When the webcast is over, send transcripts to the press.

CYBERSPACE, THE FINAL FRONTIER

The conventional means of reaching and persuading members of the media are no longer sufficient by themselves. You must also deploy

THE CONFESSIONS OF AN INK-STAINED WRETCH

> The proliferation of viewpoints on the Internet can often advance the dialogue faster than a handful of self-appointed experts, much as the thousands of participants in an economic market can make the best choice about which products are the best. To be sure, an Army of Davids is taking on the corporate Goliath.

online tools as supplements. Marketing methods must adapt to the new communications realities of cyberspace.

In-person gatherings, such as press conferences, have always been expensive for marketers to operate. Reaching reporters at trade shows, conventions and briefings entail plenty of overhead and hassle. Enter a new alternative: virtual events. The Web can be used for live and highly imaginative events to boost the impression you make with reporters.

Webcasts are a powerful means for pitching several journalists simultaneously. The same holds true for podcasts (see sidebar). Webcasts are cost-effective because they preclude the expense of direct calls and travel, and they're growing in effectiveness as web-based presentation technologies improve.

When it comes to choosing between yet another dog-and-pony show in a local pressroom, or a genuinely informative webcast on their own computers, journalists typically prefer the latter. That doesn't mean you should stop organizing or attending live events altogether, but it does mean that you should determine when a webcast would perform the same job.

CHAPTER 7: BARBARIANS AT THE GATE

The nature of the Internet is to function as an interactive community. Continual feedback from journalists attending a webcast helps you refine and hone not only your future webcasts, but also marketing collateral of all types.

Using the Internet to reach a targeted journalistic audience allows you to connect with a maximum amount of people, regardless of their location, time zone or any other constraint that entails traveling or meeting in person. When developing your press campaign, the ability to reach the widest possible audience is a big factor.

Marketing and public relations organizations have been among the leading early adopters of web-based live events. One of the advantages of using the Web is the ability to take advantage of rich media and make content more engaging, and thereby keep journalists' attention longer.

The mistaken notion still persists that web-based live events are impractical as marketing efforts because the technology still entails too many logistical problems. Several years ago, it may have been a complicated process to set up a Web event to reach hundreds of prospects. That's no longer true. New technology has worked out these bugs and made Web events easily available and manageable for marketers.

By comparison with online methods, conventional marketing is insufficiently dynamic and gets lost in the white noise — it lacks the compelling "call to action" and urgency of webcasts and podcasts. On-demand presentations are more engaging than static Web pages.

Rest assured, you don't need to be a technologist to use these solutions. Any marketing or public relations professional can hold an online webcast to engage journalists. The user friendliness of the technology is key.

THE CONFESSIONS OF AN INK-STAINED WRETCH

Email your outline to the webcast panelists ahead of time, so they're fully prepped and confident. Don't follow the script in a stilted, mechanical way. Use the script as a "safety net" to help your panelists feel comfortable, but within the script's parameters, make sure you ad lib and extemporize. It's akin to what the theatrical director Lee Strasberg would tell his students in the New York Actor's Studio: "Learn your lines, so you can forget them." This scripted method of conducting webcasts has always worked well for me.

Now, let's move from the brave new world to a world that time forgot: Congress. Here's how to get your message heard in the hallowed halls of the national legislature, as well as getting elected officials to hop aboard your promotional bandwagon.

Chapter 8

THE LAST PLANTATION

Or, How to Exploit Your Senator's Need to Pander

Perhaps your marketing strategy is to incorporate the wisdom of our nation's lawmakers. For example, you've decided that your press release would carry a lot more weight if it quoted a member of Congress who embraced your message. Better still, your press conference would generate considerably more coverage if you could convince a member to show up and participate as a speaker.

> "READER, SUPPOSE YOU WERE AN IDIOT. AND SUPPOSE YOU WERE A MEMBER OF CONGRESS. BUT I REPEAT MYSELF."
> – Mark Twain

So, you want to know: how do I get the member's attention?

THE CONFESSIONS OF AN INK-STAINED WRETCH

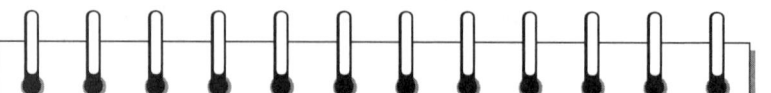

> If you work on a congressional staff, the pay is lousy and the protections are virtually non-existent. As a press secretary, your every waking moment is devoted to making the boss look good. Your job is to stroke his, or her, ego and to efface your own. If you don't quickly learn this fact of life, you're out the door. That's why Congress earns its sobriquet, "The Last Plantation."

The answer is to win over his staff, especially the press secretary. A representative or senator's job today is so complicated that they must lean on their staffers as never before. Staffers often read legislation for their bosses and tell them how to vote. Many members would be lost without their staff. Sway the staff and you've swayed the member.

During the 1950s, when the demagogue Joe McCarthy intimidated the press, and yellow columnists such as Walter Winchell routinely smeared non-conforming social critics as either communists or homosexuals, there were very few press secretaries plying their trade in Congress. As with lobbyists and political consultants, the number has since exploded. Today, nearly 800 press secretaries are milling around Capitol Hill, trying to keep busy and look important. The expansion of press secretaries is mirrored by the growth of reporters stationed in Washington by out-of-town newspapers. Roughly 1,800 reporters are registered in the daily congressional print gallery alone.

CHAPTER 8: THE LAST PLANTATION

How do you get the attention of this interrelated media machinery? By pandering to the member's incessant need to pander.

Tip O'Neill famously said, "All politics is local." Even for those rare members who enjoy a national reputation, this axiom is indeed true. I once served as a press secretary to U.S. Rep. Byron Dorgan (D-ND), now Senator. I hasten to add, Mr. Dorgan is a fine public servant, then and now. Former tax commissioner of North Dakota, Mr. Dorgan is a conscientious politician with a profound sense of right and wrong. He speaks plainly and harbors genuine empathy for common people. He isn't a liberal in the urban, blue state sense. Instead, he's a prairie populist whose innate distrust of economic concentration harks back to the New Deal populists of the Northern Midwest, who fought the rapaciousness of banks and railroad oligarchs. He's also a nice guy, a rarity in Congress.

It's not Mr. Dorgan's fault that, for most press secretaries, daily reality constitutes an absurd game of running in place. There's plenty of commotion in Congress, with little end result. Case in point: 40 percent of legislation passed by our august national legislature is in the form of a commemorative, e.g.: "Congress proclaims February to be 'Ice Cream Appreciation Month.' " Your tax dollars at work.

Members of Congress are, by necessity, parochial. When Mr. Dorgan first hired me, he warned me that he wanted his constituents back home to gradually become accustomed to me. No press release was issued, heralding my addition to the staff. "The local reporters back home in North Dakota will resent the fact that I hired an east coast city slicker like you," he told me. "They'll wonder why I didn't hire one of them and it might adversely affect the coverage we get."

THE CONFESSIONS OF AN INK-STAINED WRETCH

One day, my feet on my desk and my Brooks Brothers repp tie unfastened, the phone rang. It was a reporter from North Dakota, calling to introduce himself to me. The reporter asked me questions about my background; I obliged. I hung up the phone and thought nothing of it — until the next morning, when a perplexed and somewhat annoyed Congressman Dorgan summoned me into his imposing office. If you're a press secretary, few experiences are scarier than being summoned by the boss. I imagine it's similar to when you're a Mafia soldier and the don abruptly asks to see you. You have a sudden urge to make out your will.

In most congressional offices, the administrative assistant (AA) is the power behind the throne and runs the office. I walked into the room to find Mr. Dorgan and his AA, both grimfaced. I had only been in the job for a few days. How had I screwed up — so soon?

Wordlessly, Mr. Dorgan handed me an article. It was from a small newspaper in North Dakota. The headline: "Dorgan Hires Boston Journalist as Press Secretary."

The article went on to describe my background: attended graduate school at Boston University; served as a staff writer at *Inc.* magazine in Boston; and — worst of all — was an associate editor at *Venture* magazine, based in New York City. The headline on the article might as well have been: "Dorgan Hires Pinko Faggot Pornographer from Babylon."

The AA squinted at me like Clint Eastwood in a spaghetti western and intoned: "This looks bad." He spoke with the utmost severity, as if I had been caught red-handed, placing state secrets on microfilm in pumpkins. I apologized profusely (something that doesn't come easily to me). During my abject groveling, I admitted to Mr. Dorgan that a wily member of my own profession had sandbagged me and I should

CHAPTER 8: THE LAST PLANTATION

have known better. Mr. Dorgan's words of "comfort" will forever ring in my ears. He said, and I quote him verbatim: "Well, it's not a complete disaster."

Again, I hasten to add, Mr. Dorgan is a fine public servant. But all politics is local and the needs and sensibilities of his constituents always come first. I impart my personal anecdote to underscore an overriding point when dealing with press secretaries: all politics isn't just local — it's astonishingly parochial. Unless you've actually worked in Congress, you have no idea just how parochial.

JEZ FOLKS

Forget the impression you may get from reading *The New York Times* or *The Washington Post*. Not all press secretaries work for members who crave national attention. In fact, most congressmen don't give a fig about the national press. They're playing to publications with titles such as *The Daily Plainsman* or *The Sioux Falls Argus Leader*. Their chief concern is not glory on a national stage, but reelection. Consequently, their focus isn't on Frank Rich or David Broder, but the ink-stained wretches back home.

Ergo, the press secretary must think the same way. When I became a press secretary, I was very excited about this new avenue in my career. I had always been a political junkie; now was my chance to work in the nation's capital, to be an insider! I envisioned myself as the congressman's right-hand man. I would play Pierre Salinger to his John Kennedy. I would serve as his adviser, confidant and strategist.

Like many young men who come to Washington to get involved in politics, I was quickly disillusioned by the reality of my job. My position mostly entailed unglamorous grunt work. I faxed, photocopied,

THE CONFESSIONS OF AN INK-STAINED WRETCH

FIVE WAYS TO INFLUENCE A PRESS OFFICE

If you want a member of Congress to play ball with your marketing message, and lend his or her prestige to your press release or event, follow these five basic rules when interacting with a congressional press office:

1. ENSURE THAT THEIR BOSS LIKES YOUR RELEASE

■ If you want the congressman to accept a quote for attribution, use strong adjectives that convey the impression that he, or she, is a great leader. Don't be stingy with words such as "bold" and "visionary."

2. MAKE THEIR BOSS SEEM LIKE A BIG SHOT

■ Even though they must cater to parochial interests back home, members of Congress nonetheless like to convey the impression that they are movers and shakers on Capitol Hill. When Newt Gingrich rose to denounce Jim Wright before the cameras of C-SPAN, viewers got the impression that Newt was making impassioned speeches about Wright's corruption to a packed House of Representatives. Then one day, in a fit of pique, the Democrats demanded that C-SPAN pan its cameras around the chamber, to reveal that Gingrich was pontificating to...empty chairs.

Congress in many ways is like a Potemkin Village. Remarks in press releases that appear to have been delivered on the floor of, say, the Senate, as if the member were a stately orator like Cicero, were often merely "entered into the record." In other words, a gofer on the member's staff hands a clerk the speech and the clerk dutifully makes the speech a part of the official record. Subsequent newsletters and releases from the member's office quote the remarks, as if they were actually delivered in person on the chamber floor.

CHAPTER 8: THE LAST PLANTATION

Use the same sleight of hand in your press release, if the member will let you, and chances are, he will readily play the familiar game. Take *pro forma* quotes from the record and make them appear as if he delivered a fiery speech to an attentive Congress.

3. IMPLY THAT THEIR BOSS'S LEGISLATIVE REACH IS NATIONWIDE AND/OR GLOBAL

If you can, give the distinct impression that the press secretary's boss exerts national or worldwide influence. Use words such as "global", or toss in the names of foreign countries, when possible.

4. TIE THE ISSUE TO LOCAL INTERESTS

When I worked for Mr. Dorgan, I worked on countless press releases devoted to farmers' interests. When the Northern Great Plains was stricken by drought, every other release had the word "drought" in the headline. This is entirely appropriate; it meant that Byron was doing his job. He introduced legislation to ease the pain of farmers who were losing their livelihoods to drought. Do some homework and learn the member's major industries and contributors back home; tailor the language of your release to those interests.

For example: if you're promoting legislation on behalf of a telecom client that's intended to lower barriers to Internet access, discover who is backing the legislation. Before contacting the members, and asking their participation in your promotional campaign, conduct research and approach them with statistics concerning levels of Internet access in their home state or district. Write a press release with language that expresses how the aforementioned bill would provide much-needed and entirely egalitarian broadband access to whatever percentage of constituents currently need it. Create a ringing quote to that effect and ask the press secretary if it can be attributed to the member.

www.inkstainedconfessions.com

THE CONFESSIONS OF AN INK-STAINED WRETCH

> **5. SHOW A TASTE FOR "THE OTHER WHITE MEAT"**
> Demonstrate how your message is inextricably linked to the member's delivery of pork to constituents. A huge advantage of incumbency, of course, is the announcement of projects that create jobs back home: new highways, defense contracts, federal subsidies and the like. It may seem shameless to you, but to a member of Congress, it's just business as usual. Make the argument that, by signing on to your message, the member is demonstrating to voters that he, or she, is "working for them." For example, if your telecom client wants cable deregulation, you can make the argument that a freer market will lead to more choices and lower costs for consumers. Yada, yada, yada. You can make a convincing case for anything.

filed and edited press releases. Mr. Dorgan happened to be a fairly accomplished writer, so he insisted on writing his own press releases. I was not a press secretary; I was a secretary in charge of press.

In a lovely bit of hypocrisy, Congress used to exempt itself from many of the work rules that it imposes on other employers. If you work on a congressional staff, the pay is lousy and the protections are virtually non-existent. As a press secretary, your every waking moment is devoted to making the boss look good. Your job is to stroke his, or her, ego and to efface your own. If you don't quickly learn this fact of life, you're out the door. That's why Congress earns its sobriquet, "The Last Plantation."

Don't be intimidated by the trappings of a congressional staff job. Most staffers are self-important, preppy little shits who labor under delusions of grandeur. More than likely, their bosses are tyrants and their jobs are sheer hell. It's a young person's game. Typically, they

CHAPTER 8: THE LAST PLANTATION

come to Capitol Hill, fresh out of an Ivy League school, to work long enough on the Hill to make contacts and get their tickets punched for a more lucrative career in the private sector. Here's a rule of thumb: the degree of a press secretary's arrogance is inversely proportional to his actual importance.

To get full contact information — postal addresses, phone numbers and extensions, email addresses, home pages and staff member names and titles — for any congressional office in the U.S. House or Senate, go to www.inkstainedconfessions.com.

In the sidebar on page 148, I convey five basic rules for dealing with press secretaries.

GETTING ATTENTION

Many people get their news not directly from a news source, but second-hand, from a trusted "thought leader" in their community or among their circle of friends. You can leverage the impact of your marketing by reaching these "influentials," and one way to do it is to get a congressional imprimatur on your message.

Also be aware of what's called "astroturf" lobbying. These are faux-consumer groups designed to influence legislation. Many "independent groups" claiming to represent the public interest are actually undercover stalking horses for corporate special interests. Whatever interest your client may serve, there's bound to be groups — astroturf or otherwise — pushing those interests. Look behind the often innocuous-sounding name of groups and determine where the funding comes from. Whoever pays the bills is crafting the message. If it buttresses your goals, consider making yourself an ally of any relevant group. Use their statistics and quote their "experts."

THE CONFESSIONS OF AN INK-STAINED WRETCH

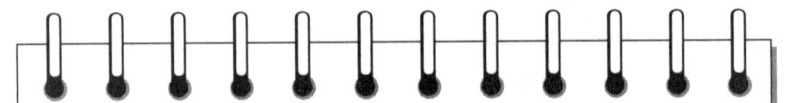

> A common mistake when trying to persuade congressional staff is to adopt a bombastic tone. The assumption is that Washington is a big debating society and a practitioner of the game must forcefully convey strong opinions to have credibility and get heard. Don't do this — it only pisses people off.

The influentials are increasingly communicating with Congress and the Internet is fueling this trend. Combined postal and email communications to the Congress exploded several hundredfold since the advent of the Internet in the mid-1990s. Taking the optimistic view, this growing interaction between citizens and congressional offices is healthy for democracy, although much of this activity is undoubtedly because it's simply easier to send email than to actually write a letter.

As a former press secretary, I can attest to the fact that there is only so much bandwidth — literally and figuratively — for a congressional office to answer the swelling tide of snail-mail and electronic correspondence. From my own experience working on the Hill, correspondence that features unique and highly individualized aspects stand a greater chance of getting attention and receiving tangible action.

Frankly, I always found that hard-copy letters that arrived in the mail made a bigger impact on the congressman and his staff — and on me. What's more, handwritten letters, as opposed to computer printouts,

CHAPTER 8: THE LAST PLANTATION

stood out the most and were the most likely to be read. Letter writing is becoming a lost art; actually getting one was a rare experience. It made people sit up and take notice.

Form letters are verboten. They're discarded faster than a dress on prom night. Also, congressional offices tend to ignore faxes more than any form of communication, because so many boring content-free faxes stream in during the day. And follow my writing rules, because there's a difference between getting noticed and actually influencing hearts and minds. Impact does not necessarily translate into influence.

A common mistake when trying to persuade congressional staff is to adopt a bombastic tone. The assumption is that Washington is a big debating society and a practitioner of the game must forcefully convey strong opinions to have credibility and get heard. Don't do this — it only pisses people off. You'll come off as a didactic blowhard and you'll get tuned out. The folks who staff congressional offices aren't a bunch of Chris Matthews wanna-bes (see Chapter Five). They're working stiffs with mortgage payments and spouses. Yes, they're politically informed and savvy, but talk to them as if they're regular people.

Matthews, pugnacious host of his own political/news slugfest on TV, once served as press secretary to the late, great Tip O'Neill, the Irish Democrat from Massachusetts who presided as Speaker of the House. Chris seems to have forgotten one of Tip's axioms. In his book, *"All Politics is Local,"* Tip writes: "Treat everyone alike — nice. Remembering that is what made my career."

As with journalists, alcohol is the social lubricant among congressional staffers in Washington. Constant fundraisers, parties, events, conferences and get-togethers combine to make the nation's capital one of the

www.inkstainedconfessions.com

THE CONFESSIONS OF AN INK-STAINED WRETCH

> A huge advantage of incumbency is the announcement of projects that create jobs back home: new highways, defense contracts, federal subsidies and the like. It may seem shameless to you, but to a member of Congress, it's just business as usual.

greatest consumers of alcohol per capita in the country. Indeed, the pressures and temptations of congressional life make alcoholism a social problem throughout Capitol Hill. Many representatives and Senators are notorious drunks and womanizers who rely on their staff for excuses, alibis and cover. (One of my favorite congressional anecdotes: when a supermarket tabloid ran a photo of a semi-naked Ted Kennedy having sex with a woman in a boat, a fellow Senator who saw the photo is reported to have remarked to Ted: "Well, I see you've changed your stance on offshore drilling.")

Regardless, my opinion is that DC nightlife has a positive effect on democracy, because it forces people to interact and know each other not as ideological combatants, but as human beings. The cocooning of America and the end-of-day flight of reporters and staffers to the suburbs have had a bad influence on the tenor of public discourse. The democratic laboratory known as Washington, DC benefits from social intercourse. We'll skip the subject of *sexual* intercourse in the capital, which has been mined all too well.

CHAPTER 8: THE LAST PLANTATION

After you get to know them a bit, invite press secretaries and attendant staffers out for drinks. Armed with a credit card and an open bar tab, you can wield considerable influence in any congressional watering hole — and by extension, influence over a congressional office.

If you're a marketer or PR professional, then by necessity, if not by definition, you must be a social animal. Don't hide behind email or the Internet. Get out of the office for face-to-face meetings. Be generous; buy gifts, drinks and meals. Always be ready with a quip. Dress sharply (but conservatively). You don't have to rival Bacchus or drink like a lush; in fact, make sure you never lose control in social situations. No one likes a loner, but by the same token, no one likes an obnoxious drunk. However, if you don't genuinely enjoy the company of others, your marketing effectiveness will be impaired — and you're probably in the wrong line of work, anyway.

In our final chapter, I'll take a look at the trends that will make the media of the future even more decentralized, and more susceptible to skilled marketing and persuasion efforts.

Chapter 9

ON THE ROAD TO ...WHERE?

How the Media Will Change Again in the Next 20 Years

Crystal ball prognostications tend to bore me. Unfortunately, the perennial "Year Ahead" article is a staple of journalism. Every December (or January), newspaper and magazine editors typically run an article, or series of articles, in which their editorial staff and a team of "experts" predict what's in store for the next 12 months.

> **"WE ARE ALL INTERESTED IN THE FUTURE, FOR THAT IS WHERE WE SHALL SPEND THE REST OF OUR LIVES."**
> – the "psychic" Criswell, in *Plan Nine From Outer Space*

THE CONFESSIONS OF AN INK-STAINED WRETCH

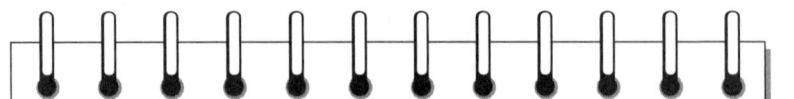

```
Print will always play a major role
in your marketing and public rela-
tions efforts. However, you must aug-
ment your efforts with new media.
RSS feeds, podcasts, webcasts, blogs
— they're no mere fads. They're here
to stay. Once considered novelties,
they're becoming commonplace. Indeed,
they're rapidly becoming expected.
```

Similarly, a "Year in Review" roundup also shows up on the calendar around the end or beginning of the year. Editors are compelled to run these articles because of routine pressure from the sales team, and the paucity of their own imaginations. Knowing these facts empowers you. Toward the end or beginning of a new year, you can tailor your story pitches accordingly.

As for prognostication clichés...well, far be it from me to part with time-honored convention. In this chapter, I discuss likely press trends of the future — to wit, further consolidation, diminished media diversity and the continued decline of newspapers — and how to capitalize on them. (In journalism, if you contradict yourself in your writing, it's not a discrepancy — we scribes like to call it a "paradox." It's a handy word that covers a lot of sins. Use it often.)

Let's start by looking not in the crystal ball, but in the rearview mirror. In 2005, the print media posted its most dismal financial performance

CHAPTER 9: ON THE ROAD TO...WHERE?

since the most recent advertising industry recession in 2000. During that particular recession, the dot-com "bust" exerted a ripple effect throughout the publishing world. Ad dollars dried up almost overnight. When the NASDAQ crashed in early 2000, the party came to a grinding halt. Publications folded or initiated drastic cutbacks. Scores of unemployed editors became ghosts peddling their resumes. The sad fact is, the media never quite bounced back from those dark days. Maybe it never will.

The immediate future for newspapers and magazines looks grim, according to cyclical factors (i.e., the state of the economy, cost of newsprint, ad spending, etc.). But the truly worrisome problems are structural and long-term.

Print media is at a tipping point, with newspapers in the most jeopardy. Jefferson may have viewed newspapers as the cornerstone of democracy, but fewer and fewer people read them. They're the least visually engaging and the least youth-oriented medium of all. The average age of a newspaper reader is roughly 55 years old.

But don't kid yourself: as I make clear in Chapter Seven, print is not dead. The key words here are "social elite." Influence trickles down from the top of the socio-economic pyramid. Maybe only a few hundred thousand people read, say, the editorial page of *The New York Times*, but that readership occupies the commanding heights of the economy and society. They exert influence far beyond their relatively small numbers.

Moreover, certain key cities — New York, Los Angeles and other "blue state" hubs — are cosmopolitan bastions that function as megaphones for the rest of the country. Regardless of print's inexorable

www.inkstainedconfessions.com

THE CONFESSIONS OF AN INK-STAINED WRETCH

FIVE GENERAL TRENDS FOR THE FUTURE

Here are the general trends I think any marketer needs to prepare for during the next few years:

1. Print will continue its inexorable decline. As a writer and someone who loves to read, this trend is particularly painful for me. But it's unstoppable, and accelerating. Newspaper circulation is dropping like a stone, magazine revenue is flat-lining, and asking a younger person (anyone under 50) to "read" something is like asking Superman to hold a piece of kryptonite. New phenomena such as Craigslist are slaughtering print classified advertising, the bedrock of revenue for many publications.

Congratulations, by the way, for joining society's intellectual elite and actually reading a book — my book. My daughter's college tuition is killing me, so I hope you paid retail for it. Which brings me to premise number two:

2. Print will never die completely. The elite — the true influencers — will always want to pick up *The Wall Street Journal* in the morning. Human nature only changes so much. (There's an expression among journalists: People who think they run the world read *The New York Times*. People who actually *do* run the world read *The Wall Street Journal*.)

decline, you've scored a major success as a marketer if you have influenced an editor at any of the major metropolitan dailies in New York or Los Angeles.

CHAPTER 9: ON THE ROAD TO...WHERE?

> Sure, video culture is dumbing down society, but 400 years after its first performance, *Romeo and Juliet* still makes people cry. Basic human nature doesn't change all that much, even over the centuries. Moreover, your target audience will always comprise the one in 10 who actually read — and think. Consequently, as I've previously explained, your marketing strategy must adopt a hybrid approach that melds old media with the new.
>
> **3. Grassroots media explodes.** Citizen journalism, in the form of bloggers, and empowered artistry, in the form of iPods, will continue chipping away at hierarchical corporate structures. Force-fed programming will go the way of radio soap operas and movie newsreels. The early 21st century will be the Era of the Amateur.
>
> Just as the printing press of the early Renaissance empowered individuals, the Internet is empowering the average person. As you craft a media strategy, never lose sight of this fragmentation. Make sure "the little guy" is invited into your conversation. At the very least, you want a snarky blogger to be inside your tent, pissing out — not outside, pissing in.

THE HYBRID STRATEGY

Print will always play a major role in your marketing and public relations efforts. However, as I've explained in this book, you must augment your efforts with new media. RSS feeds, podcasts, webcasts, blogs — they're no mere fads. They're here to stay. Once considered novelties, they're becoming commonplace. Indeed, they're rapidly becoming expected. In Chapter Seven, I explain how to exploit online communications.

THE CONFESSIONS OF AN INK-STAINED WRETCH

4. **Community media become hugely influential.** Social websites centered on particular interests will become *de facto* lobbying groups. The Internet will continue its evolution into a conversational beehive. There is a web site for every conceivable interest, niche, hobby or proclivity, whether it's for media oversight, political ideologues, beekeepers or Swedish biker chicks that dig leather (the latter being the most compelling, or course). My Larstan colleague Jason Van Orden, an experienced podcast producer, offers particularly useful insights into social web sites and podcasting, in his trenchant books, "Podcasting 101" and "Promoting Your Podcast" (http://www.PodcastingUniversity.org).

5. **Cell phones become integrated into media.** People may be getting dumber, but your cell phone will keep getting smarter. Mobile phones will increasingly incorporate video, text, photography and all sorts of multi-media functionality. I remember, on a trip to Finland (home to cell phone giant Nokia), I saw my host use his cell phone to pay his parking meter and get a soda from a vending machine. He did everything with his cell phone but shave with it. Converged cell phone functionality will become less of a novelty and more pervasive.

Indeed, online communications are on track for explosive growth. RSS news feeds, podcasts, blogs and webcasts will play an increasingly powerful role in marketing, for years to come. According to Wainhouse Research, a Boston-based communications research and consulting firm that specializes in "rich media," the demand for online, rich-media presentations will grow at a compound rate of 90 percent a year, for the next three years.

CHAPTER 9: ON THE ROAD TO...WHERE?

You should take advantage of cross-channel synergies to leverage your message. Remember: the Web should be used to enhance your print-based message, not obviate it. Deploy an integrated marketing communications strategy. If your message is inherently weak and you can't create a coherent press release, launching flashy Internet gimmicks won't bail you out. You'll just fail faster. By the same token, as I explain below, you don't want to come off as an Internet illiterate. With technology, strike a balance between winsome confidence and off-putting geekiness. In the words of Nigel Tufnel, lead guitarist for Spinal Tap: "It's a fine line between clever and stupid."

THE VIRTUAL COMMUNITY

People tend to gravitate toward those who are like-minded. One of the worst qualities of journalists is their parochial nature when it comes to relationships.

Those with common interests create "virtual communities" by establishing web-based chat rooms, bulletin boards, newsletters, e-zines and online clubs. For example, Yahoo sponsors chat rooms for all kinds of topics, ranging from books to movies to politics to sex. As I've reiterated throughout this book, focus is everything. That's why the emergence of the highly focused virtual community is an opportunity for you. Always consider targeting these groups, through their respective e-zines and online periodicals.

The United States is the most Internet-literate nation on earth, representing about 40 percent of the online consumer market. That will change in the coming years. Analysts predict that the Western European market is poised to at least pull even with the U.S., and the fast-growing Asia-Pacific economies will outpace both markets by the end of this decade.

THE CONFESSIONS OF AN INK-STAINED WRETCH

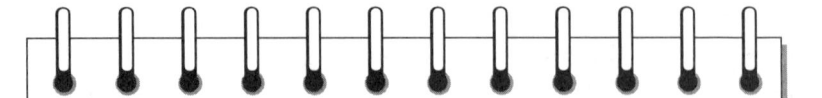

```
Citizen journalism, in the form of
bloggers, and empowered artistry, in
the form of iPods, will continue
chipping away at hierarchical corpo-
rate structures. Force-fed program-
ming will go the way of radio soap
operas and movie newsreels.
```

FUTURE SCHLOCK

The great futurist Alvin Toffler wrote a seminal book, *Future Shock*, published in 1970, that widely influenced society. Indeed, the title entered the language as a sociological term. His book is more applicable than ever.

The basic premise of the book is that many social ills are symptoms of the failure of individuals and organizations to cope with rapidly accelerating social and technological change. People are threatened and disoriented by this change and yearn for a return to simpler times — halcyon days that never really existed. A yearning for a bygone and romanticized "golden era" is a familiar phenomenon in human history, but it's particularly acute today as the Information Age throws many comforting assumptions into the dustbin.

The fact is, many people prefer to run from freedom, because taking responsibility for your own life and facing the inherent messiness of the human condition is too frightening. It's far easier to place your fate

CHAPTER 9: ON THE ROAD TO...WHERE?

into the hands of a Big Daddy, whether that daddy lives in a national capital or in the sky.

Toffler's more recent book, *The Third Wave*, also proved influential — and prescient. He posited the notion that human society has undergone three major paradigm-shifts. The first wave represents humankind's transition from nomadic hunter-gatherer to farmer. Agriculture and attendant villages appeared; civilization was born. The second wave marks the rise of machines, industrialization and mass culture. The third wave — well, you're riding it, buddy. It's the Information Age — computers, the Internet, bioengineering, virtual offices, etc.

Here's my point: worlds are colliding. To thrive as a marketer in today's environment, you need to possess an existential attitude. In other words, deal with things the way they are, not the way you wish them to be. To broach evolution again: you must adapt, or die. Pretty-sounding verities are just a bunch of sentimental schlock. To cope with bewildering change, you must wake up every morning prepared to be astonished, and to respond accordingly.

As you deal with journalists, remember that they're like sharks. You don't have to like them, but they need to be fed on a regular basis. Also, remember that they sometimes get whipped into a feeding frenzy, whereupon they start eating other sharks — and even their own guts.

All contacts with the media are useful, even those that are ostensibly minor. Conversations, emails, voicemails, faxes — every interaction is a bit of personal karma that you're throwing out into the media cosmos. Eventually, some of that karma will return to benefit you. (And you thought I wasn't a spiritual guy!) Repetition is crucial. You never plateau, you never "arrive" and you never develop tenure. As with

THE CONFESSIONS OF AN INK-STAINED WRETCH

> Many social ills are symptoms of the failure of individuals and organizations to cope with rapidly accelerating social and technological change. People are threatened and disoriented by this change and yearn for a return to halcyon days that never really existed.

Sisyphus and his rock, your endeavors are ceaseless. (Hopefully, your endeavors won't be as pointless.)

The same holds true for the media relationships you develop. You should nurture them over the long haul, but today's hero can quickly become tomorrow's goat. Alliances change as enemies become friends, and vice versa. Nothing remains stationary. A reporter may love you one day and, for some inexplicable reason, treat you like a schmuck the next.

Train your mind to detect media opportunities, and get in the habit of reflexively jumping on them. Unexpected chances to manipulate the media will spring up every day. Those chances are serendipitous gifts; don't pass them up. Show clients and the media that you're a savvy practitioner in the post-industrial era. Actually, in light of the Internet, it appears that we're now in the "post" post-industrial era.

CHAPTER 9: ON THE ROAD TO...WHERE?

You don't have to drop techno-jargon and act like a geeky propeller head, because that's just plain annoying. But demonstrate your computer and Internet savvy. Become a "cyber player." The more you actually use these computer skills, the more proficient you'll become and the more insights you'll develop for exerting influence on the media. As I posited earlier, marketing bullshit permeates everything. Paradoxically, journalists and other influencers can smell a phony a mile away. If you appear clumsy or uninformed with Internet basics, you'll be written off faster than lunch at a Manhattan restaurant.

Above all, hang in there. In October 1941, when the global situation appeared bleak and England was the only bulwark against Nazi barbarism, Winston Churchill gave a speech to the boys at Harrow School. His words still put a lump in my throat: "Never give in, never give in, never, never, never, never — in nothing, great or small, large or petty — never give in except to convictions of honour and good sense."

The only constant is change; your greatest weapon in an uncertain world is perseverance. As you soldier on in your marketing efforts, you might require additional advice. Don't hesitate to drop me a line at jpersinos@larstan.net. Or visit www.inkstainedconfessions.com.

Develop a thick skin. In today's turbulent society, it's absurd to take rejection personally. Your life has been reduced to a swirling, amoral miasma of 1s and 0s. Learn to navigate that miasma — with speed, agility and, dare I say it, grace.

THE CONFESSIONS OF AN INK-STAINED WRETCH

INDEX

Spiro Agnew	73
Martin Agronsky	94
Alcoa	85
alcohol	153
AOL Time Warner	22, 35
Michael Barone	127
Basecamp	130
bloggers	126, 130
blogs	161
Robert Bork	29
Boston University	10
Ben Bradlee	45
David Broder	147
Pat Buchanan	75
George W. Bush	9, 29
Campaigns & Elections	101
Andrew Card	9
Winston Churchill	38, 167
Johnny Cochran	73
Bill Clinton	29
CNN	94
Congress	13, 17, 143, 145, 148, 150, 152
Craigslist	160
Walter Cronkite	32
C-SPAN	148
Disney	22
Byron Dorgan	145, 146, 147, 149, 150
Matt Drudge	19, 28
Entertainment Tonight	31
ExxonMobil	56

www.inkstainedconfessions.com

THE CONFESSIONS OF AN INK-STAINED WRETCH

FCC	21
Fox News	28
David Frost	113
Future Shock	164
General Electric	22, 27
Newt Gingrich	148
Google	12, 122
Harper's	94
Health Maintenance Organizations (HMOs)	37
William Randolph Hearst	32
Internet	122, 124, 126, 132, 134, 139, 152
interviews	108, 110, 111, 116
inverted pyramid	63
iPods	161
Steve Jobs	15
A.J. Liebling	12
Lowell Sun	13
John Kennedy	81, 147
Joseph Kennedy	109
Ketchum Inc.	57
John Kerry	28
Michael Kinsley	75, 94
Henry Kissinger	11
Macromedia	131
managing editor	47
Chris Matthews	153
Joe McCarthy	144
George McGovern	73
John McLaughlin	93
MP3	136
MTV	19
Rupert Murdoch	28

THE CONFESSIONS OF AN INK-STAINED WRETCH

New Yorker	14
News Corp.	22
newsletter companies	117
newspapers	159, 160
Richard Nixon	79, 94, 113
David Ogilvy	61
Ken Olson	121
Podcasting	129, 136, 137, 161
press releases	131, 148
press secretary	144, 155
punditry	95, 104
Dan Rather	127
Ronald Reagan	104
Sumner Redstone	43
Regnery	28
Reporters	27, 47, 49, 81, 144
Glenn Reynolds	125
Scotty Reston	56
Frank Rich	147
John D. Rockefeller	35
Karl Rove	29, 107
RSS	127, 129, 130, 161
William Safire	56, 73
Pierre Salinger	147
Orville Schell	125
Herb Schmertz	55
Silicon Valley	15
O.J. Simpson	73
Slate	94
Al Smith	73
sound bite	73
Jerry Springer	19
St. Anthony's Publishing	34
story calendar	50
Swift Boat Veterans for Truth	28
syndication	127, 130

THE CONFESSIONS OF AN INK-STAINED WRETCH

tabloid journalism 45
talk shows 103
television 27, 93, 95, 99
The Lowell Sun 43
The New Republic 94
The New York Times 9, 122, 147, 159, 160
The Orlando Sentinel 13, 32, 37
The Third Wave 165
The Wall Street Journal 160
The Washington Post 147
Alvin Toffler 164
Boss Tweed 70
TypePad 130

USAToday 13

Viacom 22
Vivendi Universal 22

Wainhouse Research 162
Mike Wallace 115
Webcasts 131, 133, 138, 161
WebEx 131
George Will 104
Armstrong Williams 57
Brian Williams 27
Walter Winchell 144
Tom Wolfe 15
Jim Wright 148

Yahoo 12, 163

WANT THE SECRETS?

GET THEM DIRECTLY FROM THE EXPERTS

AVAILABLE AT BOOKSTORES EVERYWHERE

Get the first chapter FREE.
Email: freechapter@theblackbooks.com
Please specify which title you want.

LARSTAN
PUBLISHING
WWW.LARSTAN.COM

THE CONFESSIONS OF AN INK-STAINED WRETCH

THE PODCAST

The weekly radio show that reveals the secrets to working with the media to get press for your business, organization or cause.

Listen or download from www.inkstainedconfessions.com

Free Show Subscription
To subscribe send your email address to wretchpodcast@larstan.net

Show Host – John Persinos

On Air

THE CONFESSIONS OF AN INK-STAINED WRETCH

ABOUT THE AUTHOR

John Persinos has enjoyed a long career in the media. He has served as a staff reporter on daily metropolitan newspapers, including *The Lowell (Mass.) Sun* and *The Orlando (Fla.) Sentinel*. He has worked on several national magazines, specifically as a staff writer at *Inc.;* an associate editor of *Venture;* managing editor of *Campaigns & Elections;* and editor-in-chief of *Rotor & Wing*. John also served as a press secretary to U.S. Rep. (now Senator) Byron Dorgan (D-ND).

John is the recipient of numerous journalistic awards, including the Royal Aeronautical Society's prestigious "Aerospace Journalist of the Year Award" in 2001, in the category of "Best General Aviation Submission," for his work on *Rotor & Wing*. He has co-authored a book, *Boston: In a Class by Itself.*

He holds a B.A. in English, an M.A. in English Literature, and an M.S. in Journalism, all from Boston University. He also completed the Davenport Fellowship in Business and Economics Reporting at the University of Missouri (Columbia) School of Journalism.

John currently serves as editorial director of Larstan Publishing, Inc., a multi-media publishing company. He lives in Barrington, Rhode Island.